LEARNING MY NAME

Also by Pete Gall

My Beautiful Idol

LEARNING MY NAME

PETE GALL

ZONDERVAN.com/
AUTHORTRACKER
follow your favorite authors

ZONDERVAN

Learning My Name
Copyright © 2009 by Peter D. Gall

This title is also available as a Zondervan ebook. Visit www.zondervan.com/ebooks.

This title is also available in a Zondervan audio edition. Visit www.zondervan.fm.

Requests for information should be addressed to:
Zondervan, *Grand Rapids, Michigan* 49530

ISBN 978-0-310-28390-4

Cover design by Mark Arnold
Author photo by MaryBeth Jackson
Interior design by Beth Shagene

Printed in the United States of America

09 10 11 12 13 14 15 • 23 22 21 20 19 18 17 16 15 14 13 12 11 10 9 8 7 6 5 4 3 2 1

For my whole family,
by whom I am loved better than I know.

CONTENTS

A Word from the Author's Father

For the most part, we don't really follow God.

Instead, we tend to build our lives around what we think we know of God and what we think he thinks of us. If we conclude that God is a frustrated taskmaster who is disappointed in our performance, we may build lives of external performance and achievement. If we fall into the logic that says God is focused on the minutiae of the law, we may become tyrants of doctrine. If it seems to us that God only comes through when we try extra hard, we may develop habits that keep us chasing dramatic displays instead of seeing God in the everyday. Conversely, if we conclude that God is love, but we also believe that love can exist without a distinct and personal God, we may build lives of mere emotionalism that leave no room for the living God of the Bible. Sometimes, we may conclude that God cares more about his big picture plan than about our individual lives. Or we may come to believe that all he really wants us to care about is how we manage the details of our own immediate lives. Whatever we conclude, our lives often end up built around what we think of God, and less around who he really is and what he may actually think of us.

What a loss that is, to live in relationship with our religion instead of our God.

It's not uncommon for us to experience the same sort of loss in our relationships with people. We have similar communication breakdowns with people all the time. We think we express our love clearly. We think we do the right things. We think everything is going along well, and then once in a while we get a glimpse of how our own failings, and the broken places in the other person, have led the relationship to exactly the wrong conclusions.

That is what this book is about. Actually, it is about undoing wrong conclusions and about clarifying what is real. This book is about turning to face the ugly, sickening moments of failure and perceived failure, and about giving up the vows we make in response to our pain.

There are stories included in this book that aren't recorded the way I remember them, or are told with the accent placed on Pete's perspective instead of mine. There are some missing facts. There are some stories that I don't remember at all. There are certainly stories I wish Pete didn't remember. I wish that there was less pain in my son's world. I wish that he had been able to tell me what he was feeling when the stories were being lived. I wish that he had chosen to interact with the real me instead of the me he thought he knew. I wish he'd asked what I actually thought about him, instead of spending years being tyrannized by the caricature of me that grew, vow by vow, in his mind.

What a loss it is, to learn late in life that your son has spent so much time relating to his ideas of you when the real you has been present, wanting nothing more than to pour love into him.

The Bible talks about the "sins of the fathers" being passed to their sons for generations. To be sure, I have passed faulty ways of relating and faulty ways of thinking to my son, just as faulty tendencies were passed to me, and so back into the fog of family history. How much has been lost in our family because of this? In every family? How much has the family of Christ lost in the same ways? How many times has my heavenly Father seen me choose the caricature of him over the real him? And how much more unfair are we to God, who has no baggage, no fallen heritage, nothing upon which to build a just, if faulty, caricature?

Unjust and unfair though they may be, there are reasons we build caricatured versions of God. There are moments of pain for us. Moments when we don't get our way, and we do not understand the reasons for our pain or for our longing. God makes hard choices, and he withstands our outbursts and our vilification of him because he loves us and because he knows what is right.

And that is where Christianity shines like no other religion; the moment when God speaks, and then holds his children while they cry and argue and shake their fists at him. While it is absolutely his prerogative to demand complete and immediate obedience and submission without regard to how his commands impact us, our God is willing to "take it on the chin" for the sake of being in relationship with his children. Our God invites it. Our God runs to greet the returning prodigal. Our God speaks with Moses. He wrestles with Jacob. He calls David a man after his own heart.

He holds his weeping Son, the one who begs as no one has ever begged, for the cup to pass in the garden at Gethsemane, and still he makes the hard decision because he loves and because he knows what is right.

And then, several brutal hours later, his Son, his sweet, beloved

Son, cries out for all the world to hear, "Father! Father! Why have you forsaken me?"

Our Father takes it on the chin because his love for his Son compels him to do so.

This is what fathers do. And this invitation to relationship, this willingness to pay for love, this is how the curses that pass from one generation to the next are reversed to become the blessings that pass from one generation to the next.

This is how we choose what is real, and this is how we choose the Trinity that is the source of love.

DAVID GALL
Zionsville, Indiana, 2008

Religion is the sigh of the oppressed creature, the heart of a heartless world, just as it is the spirit of a spiritless situation. It is the opium of the people. The abolition of religion as the illusory happiness of the people is required for their real happiness. The demand to give up the illusion about its condition is the demand to give up a condition which needs illusions.

KARL MARX, *CRITIQUE OF HEGEL'S PHILOSOPHY OF RIGHT*

In Search of a More Pleasant Opiate

Most days I'm not looking for an omnipotent God. I don't need all-powerful. Just a little potent, say medium powerful, will do.

I have a few complaints and a few broken places that snowball into chronic problems, but nothing a deity can't snap into place. I'm just looking for a little heavenly chiropractic care. Most days, a merely potent God would be plenty for me.

But even with my lowered expectations, God isn't showing up to fix me the way I'd like him to — even when I scrunch up my face and pray real hard. He doesn't repair me when I go to church, when I see my counselor, when I confess and repent. Even when I really mean it. He doesn't set me on my feet and make me whole when I attend my recovery meetings, even if I keep coming back because "it works if I work it and I work it because I'm worth it."

And I do keep coming back, but I'm still broken in the same places. I know he's there, and it's like I keep telling him about some metaphorical femur that's jutting out from my broken thigh, but he simply isn't doing that holy bonesetter thing I'm looking for from him.

So here I wait, with no idea where else I could go. I'm left with the weak comfort of words like *obedience* and *diligence* and *endurance*. And ... *perseverance*? Fine, he can have my perseverance. I'll keep dragging myself along and we'll call it perseverance, but I'd be so much more valuable to the world if I could get a little help with my broken places. I promise I'd still show up at church from time to time, or whatever.

I'm lonely. I'm scared. I don't know what to do with my life. I fail at things. I quit on things even when I swear that I'll stick to them. I have addictions that rule me. I'm addicted to compulsive eating, to control, to shame, to what you think of me. I'm broken in those places, and others, and still others that I don't even know about yet.

And trying harder isn't making things better. I'm not looking to raise someone from the dead, and I'm not looking to move a mountain. I just want to stop when I've had enough. I want to trust my life. I want to believe that God's love is real, and sufficient. I want to be able to tell you the truth about me without trying too hard. And I want to let that be all right with me. Nothing huge, you know? Just your ordinary miracles.

But nothing I do seems to get God's attention for him to come fix me. Nothing I plug away at — no discipline or meditation or "hard truth" — seems to do anything other than cinch my pain tighter, making me feel even more like a waste for my brokenness.

I know I'm not alone in this. I also know I'm not alone in my persistent belief that there's got to be a workable life within my faith somewhere. Maybe it's hidden under all of the failed promises I've heard from church leaders who tell me I'll feel better if I just try harder, but whose counsel has left me worse off, and feeling farther from God than ever.

Christianity has been no opiate to me. In fact, the Christianity I've learned would be better described as the salt in the wounds of the people. I don't feel better, and I *should* feel better.

If I don't risk asking the hard questions soon, and if I don't get some peace with the answers I find, I'll be lost. I mean, I'll be dead. I will die from my addictions. I will die miserable. And others will be made miserable by my passing (or by the guilt they'll feel for experiencing relief that I'm finally gone).

I hurt, and I'm tired of hurting. I believe, but my faith is crumbling in the oven of my reality, and I have no choice but to take another look at the guts of this religion, desperate to find something new there. The fantasy version of my life — the one I shine up especially bright with effort and decorum and caveat and principles for the Christians — isn't working anymore.

Maybe Karl Marx has a point, whether it was his intended point or not. Maybe there really is something to be said for abolishing illusory happiness for the sake of real happiness. Maybe it's time for me to give up my illusions about my condition, in hopes of giving up a condition that needs illusions to make it survivable.

Life should feel better than this. *I* should feel better than this.

DISCUSSION QUESTIONS

1. What do you believe happens when you ask for God's forgiveness?

2. What do you *feel* after you ask for God's forgiveness?

3. What do you believe happens when you ask for God's healing?

4. What do you *feel* after you ask for God's healing?

5. Is there a different purpose for forgiveness than healing, or do our efforts to address both sin and suffering lead to the same place with God?

PART I

THE RUB

CHAPTER 1

CHRISTIANITY'S CASH COW

Books on grace sell huge to Christian audiences because so much of Christian culture has an incredible ability to make people feel like failures for their ordinary imperfections. In the light of what is commonly experienced in Christian culture, grace sounds like this sweet "get out of jail free" card I can play when I'm left with no other option but to admit defeat and look for the magical way out.

Ultimately, it's not the books on grace that make me feel like a failure, and the problem is certainly not grace. The problem is not the churches or the Christian industries that generate a mixed bag of worthy and unworthy products; they're just a reflection of the market. The problem is not even the Fall. After all, sin will continue to exist alongside redemption in this world — wheat mingled with chaff, sheep hanging out with goats — and Jesus said nothing could separate us from him. Truth be told, my sin isn't what makes me feel like a failure. What makes me feel so lousy is the lens through which I see myself and the meaning of my sin. The problem is woven deep within the fabric of how I see the world, and it has everything to do with my ongoing refusal to truly — even indolently — allow myself to be loved by God.

Philip Yancey, one of the foremost authors on grace, includes this pearl in one of his books: "We're all bastards, but God loves us anyhow."[1] I want to find comfort with both halves of that sentiment. I want to be as okay with my fallen state as God seems to be, and I want to let God do the work of shaping me with his love.

Martin Luther, the booming voice of grace in the history of the Protestant church, understood something huge about our bastardly ways and sin's inability to drive the love of God away from us when he wrote:

> If you are a preacher of grace, then preach a true and not a fictitious grace; if grace is true, you must bear a true and not a fictitious sin. God does not save people who are only fictitious sinners. *Be a sinner and sin boldly, but believe and rejoice in Christ even more boldly, for he is victorious over sin, death, and the world.* As long as we are here [in this world] we have to sin. This life is not the dwelling place of righteousness but, as Peter says, we look for new heavens and a new earth in which righteousness dwells. It is enough that by the riches of God's glory we have come to know the Lamb that takes away the sin of the world. No sin will separate us from the Lamb, even though we commit fornication and murder a thousand times a day. Do you think that the purchase price that was paid for the redemption of our sins by so great a Lamb is too small? Pray boldly — you too are a mighty sinner. (emphasis added)[2]

St. Augustine, whose impact on Christianity can hardly be

overstated, was maybe even more willing to let go of the fear of failure and risk humanity's mess to the care of the love of God when he preached about how to deal with sinners and said, "And if you shout at him, love him inwardly; you may urge, wheedle, rebuke, rage; *love, and do whatever you wish*" (emphasis added).[3]

I don't want to be broken. I hate the sin within me, and I do want God to reshape me. But when I look to people like Augustine, Luther, and Yancey, it doesn't take long before I see that maybe I focus more on my sins than on God's love for me. Something is broken with the way I interact with the world and with my sin, and it costs me the experience of God's love. It leaves me trapped in my own fallen state. I want to experience the healing and freedom — in addition to the forgiveness — of God's love.

I am coming to have this feeling that for all of us, in one way or another, God eventually lets the pressures of our sins pile up against our best efforts and most ardent attempts at faith so that we crumble, throw in the towel, and give the bastardly parts of ourselves to God to do with as he will.

And that is where the adventure begins.

LINGERING IN FRIDAY

The adventure is not about the finished, cleaned-up moral version of who I am, either. The adventure is about experiences that teach me who God is, and who I am in relation to him. It's no trick to tell us apart: I'm the weepy broken one, and he's the one who can't stop laughing from the delight he feels in my company.

One source of ongoing struggle for me is that I'm really bad at "lingering in Friday." For me, Christianity fails when in my haste and selfishness I fixate on a life of Easter Sundays, all victorious and pastel-clad, and I forget that the place where I was first afforded space in the embrace of God was on Good Friday at the foot of the Cross. Good Friday is where I return over and over, filthy and foolish and burdened by my failures, and where I see how God loves me anyway. Not in a way that ignores my dirt, but in a way that seems to almost value the dirt, because the dirt is what brings me to him. Good Friday is where I see the difference between myself and my sin. I think I would feel better if I spent more time lingering in Friday. And I bet my image of God would change a lot too.

But Friday was an ugly scene. We run into some pretty unsavory characters at the foot of the Cross — at their most unsavory. The drunk is still drunk. The adulterer still smells like perfume and sweat and whatever else. The envious neighbor looks us up and down, checking our clothes for brand names. And behind them, a million other people crowd around, every one sobbing and snotty in utter brokenness. That's the truth of this kingdom of ours, and it's beautiful; but it doesn't package well and it doesn't translate to television for jack.

Friday is the height of Jesus' glory, because that is when the Godhead opens a space for us to be brought into the love that flows between the Father, Son, and Spirit. It's when the curtain in the temple dividing the holy from the unholy rips, from the top down. The power and the love of the Lord is unveiled, and it is majestic. It's majestic for God. But Friday is also the day the lights come on in a dark world full of sinners who've come to believe they own the place. Good Friday is the worst day in the long and storied history of Adam's stolen glory, because it was the day our stolen glory truly died.

I'm embarrassed about the mess and ugliness of Good Friday. I hate how I was. How, to my chagrin, I still am — even if in lesser or different ways. I've experienced enough of my own need for the Cross that I tend to feel pretty sure I can't trust a person who's on their way up *that* hill; I know what depravity exists in people who go there. Those people have "issues." I don't want to be lumped in with them. I don't want to pay the social cost I'm sure to pay if other people see me in my desperate need and brokenness. Besides, the Cross was "once and for all," right? It's finished, right? We can't crucify him again, right?

It's kind of gauche, and certainly not appropriate for mixed company, to dwell upon the Cross. We've been forgiven, set free, loosed, named more than conquerors. It's time to figure out what's next and get on with it. To God be the glory — leave the snapshots from Golgotha in the closet.

It doesn't work, does it? As dutiful Christians who've come to believe that Jesus only heals all at once and often only to the level of our faith, many of us refuse to give each other permission to admit it yet, but the embarrassing truth is that we need to return to the Cross again and again, even if it's only a brief visit under the cover of night or because a profound momentary crisis drives us to cry out for Christ's mercy once more.

We are powerless against our sin. It has seeped into our bodies and become a disease. The filth returns. We still eat too much, or lust too much, or drink too much, or control too much, or put ourselves in harm's way in a nearly infinite variety of ways. We will forever stumble back into the need for the Cross, whether it's for salvation or relief from our burdens. The horrible bottom-line truth is that the Cross is the only place where we make sense.

WHAT DOESN'T WORK

I think Christians gobble up books on grace because the books give us permission to experience a love that's happy to see us even if we arrive absolutely covered in our failures. We're desperate for any bits of comfort about grace because the best our Christianity has been able to say to us about our failures — much like a football coach yelling to his players on a hot day in training camp — is to go grab a cup of grace, then come back and redouble our efforts.

This much I do know: You will not get better at this because you try harder. You will not get better at this because you double down on your bets. You will not get better at this, and continuing to tell yourself otherwise will only drive the pain deeper. You will continue to move from personal failure to personal failure, church disappointment to church disappointment, drama to drama. And at the end of a long trail of what will surely feel like dutiful searching for wisdom and the application of right answers, the time will come when this whole thing will break in thorough, painful, irrevocable fashion. On that day you will have to decide who lied about your pain and the ways you responded to it. The answer you'll have to confront is that it was you — you lied — and you were lied to, and you worked in concert with the liars to ride the lies as far as you could.

But it'll be much easier to blame the breaking on God. Or to give up on him. Or to walk away from church, blaming the jokers whose advice only made matters worse. And if you're like me, that'll be what you do.

That won't work either. Maybe you already know it, though I pray you know it from wisdom rather than experience. Walk away from God and his Church, and after a while the quiet moments catch up with you. The small confessions. The small admissions. The small truths. The flickering evidence of a good thing discarded. At some point you see that you lied to yourself and that you chose the words of liars over the counsel of the Lord.

You'll have to figure out just how the wording of the lies strings out in your world, but the truth I think you'll find — the truth I think

I'm finding — is this: Easter Sunday looks good on TV, but it belongs to Jesus.

Good Friday is for us. And it is good.

"GOOD" FRIDAY

On Good Friday, because Jesus takes the lower, more accursed position than ours, reaching deeper into — and overcoming — sin to make room for our sin within the loving relationship between Father and Son, we're afforded a new identity and a new safety in the merciful love of our Lord. That makes Good Friday the day that's most profoundly ours, however disgusting and deeply humbling the pain that drives us there may be. And we know it's an invitation to a divine relationship, where all glory is reflected to another, because even though the day is ours, we never gain control over it. We're not the stars. The star is Jesus, human and dying tragically with an invitation for us to heap all of our mess upon him as he goes, and to thereby cast our fate — namely what will become of us for the rottenness we feel within ourselves — into his care.

Good Friday is the day we are taken into the embrace of the God over and against whom we've previously forged our identity. Until Good Friday, we know ourselves only as independent beings. We measure ourselves independently, with thoughts of God being somewhere "out there," removed and distant. Until Good Friday, we live an absurd illusion as created beings, somehow convinced that a created being can make sense on its own, independent from a creator. Until Good Friday, we are bullets who deny the existence of a gun. We are echoes who deny the existence of a voice. We are children who deny the existence of parents. Until Good Friday, we live an irrational lie that argues independence from a God upon whom we are wholly dependent.

On Good Friday we experience dependence. That doesn't mean we experience the elimination of self. It means we experience the ultimate harmony that comes to created beings when they yield themselves up to their Creator. We remain, but whatever irrational evidence we've used to measure our independent selves in the past disappears. On Good Friday, the only context we know is personal and immediate and eternal, complete and without gradient. On that day we experience ourselves within the context of God's delighting, laughing, whole, and all-powerful love.

On Good Friday, we see our true selves for the first time, and we cannot help but respond. On Good Friday, we finally make sense. We see that we do not have to continue berating ourselves for our failures because the whole idea of independent success is absurd within the context of God's embrace. Within the relationship of the Godhead, there is no failure. There is no success. There is only God and his searching love, always present and complete and encompassing. The world falls into place, and the world is good. On Good Friday we finally sigh, soul deep, and relax into the love of God.

THEN THE CHRISTIANS SHOW UP

And then, if you respond like so many of the good Christian people tell you to, you'll close your eyes, raise your hand, stand up, come down to the altar, pray the prayer, receive the applause, shuffle to the anteroom to get the photocopied handbooks, plug in to a small group, have your daily "quiet time," read watery books until you start reading convoluted books full of insider terminology, volunteer to do some good deeds, attend church regularly, maybe start leading a new small group, take missions trips once or twice a year, tell your co-workers about the four laws or seven principles or five secrets that begin with the letter "c," and you'll obsess on your new found job of demonstrating how the mostly grotesque and shameful moment of Good Friday has flowered into a lifetime of Easter Sundays, ripe for testimony. And you'll never risk truly sighing, soul deep, and relaxing into the love of God again. And when you die, you'll jog off life's football field, and the coach will pat you on the back and say, "Well done, good and faithful linebacker — go grab some Gatorade."

The problem isn't that the stuff the Christians tell you to do is wrong. The problem is that the stuff so many Christians focus on is so astoundingly weak compared to the majesty of the Cross. The problem is that the Cross is treated like some cut-rate warm-up act for the programs and agendas and sermon series the Christians are *really* excited about. The problem is that there is so much more, and so many of us spend most of our lives missing it.

Christians experience comfort from God. But Christians *are* Christians because of Good Friday. Good Friday is where *our* miracles happen, where our lives engage the rest of the world, where our identity is continually shaped. The changes we experience — the changes that are the real Easter in our lives — take place because we live the Friday of our brokenness all the way...

Then we live the Saturday of our submission and yielded healing all the way...

Then the Sunday of changed life happens because that's the way the week unfolds.

You cannot live Sunday until you've lived Friday and Saturday. If Christians rarely experience the love of God in lasting ways, it may have something to do with how nearly impossible it is to live Friday and Saturday in the Christian culture. We're too busy making Jesus — and ourselves — look good, and we end up so fixated on

Sunday that we don't really let Good Friday sink in. To the extent that we gloss over Good Friday, we remain mystified about our true identity, our true context. All too often we live our lives from a merely functional — as opposed to relational — partial understanding of ourselves and our lives.

This is the part that has been breaking for me, this merely functional sense of self and faith. This is the part that I hope will break for you too.

HEAD GAMES AND "FUNCTIONALITY"

Back in the days of the early Church, there was a group of people who believed that Jesus was not fully human, that he only seemed to be human, like he was a ghost wearing a meat suit or something. They were called the Docetists, from the Greek word *dokeo*, which means "to seem."

This approach fit into a larger philosophy called Gnosticism. The name comes from the Greek word *gnosis*, which means "knowledge." The Gnostics believed that knowledge was the key. They believed in a clear split between the physical body and the rest of what we are, and they believed that the body was a lousy thing. They believed that the path to God involved getting past the body and more or less following layers of understanding to the big ultimate truth. They referred to the created world as "emanations" of an ultimate truth. They believed you could follow those emanations back to the ultimate source — sort of like how you can figure out where the rock hit the pond's surface if you follow the ripples, or emanations, back to the center.

For the Gnostics and the Docetists, the important thing was the nonphysical self — the mind and the will. Those aspects of ourselves were considered good, or at least potentially good. But the body and the appetites, both physical appetites and other appetites, like the appetite we have to be known and loved, were fallen or sinful. That's why the Docetists couldn't make room for Jesus to be fully human. To their way of thinking, that would mean he was also fallen.

For them the key to getting your mess cleaned up had to do with growing the mind and will, and shrinking the fallen physical self. If you could pull your unfallen mental self apart from the appetites of your fallen self, you could get enough clarity to discipline your whole self and clean things up.

PUTTING OURSELVES TOGETHER

I mention the Docetists and the Gnostics because I see their perspective in full bloom all over the place in Christianity today. Modern, postmodern, Evangelical, Reformed, Catholic, liberal, conservative. Even when we don't make any sense at all, we're still stuck in our heads, and we're terrified of the rest of who we are. We hide what we can't control, and we cheat the world by insisting that we have right answers even though we can't show how we reached those conclusions. I think today's Church is more dedicated to the Enlightenment — whose many attempts to correct a superstitious and abusive religious presence mostly drove us back to a Gnostic rationality — than we are to Scripture or the God of Good Friday (and all the other days).

We don't need to live this way. The rock that hit the pond — the God who is the ultimate source of the emanations — still inhabits a physical Jewish body and also inhabits the physical lumpy bodies of those who will have him. God is not "out there." God is closer than your next thought, your next breath, or your deepest yearning.

31

We do not have to scrunch up our faces in some ecstatic attempt to prayerfully escape this place to find our way to God. God is more than willing to play on our turf. Our part is to let God come to us. His passion is not to be understood, but to be *known*. There is a big difference.

God has chosen my body as the "ground of meeting" for my relationship with him, as I believe he has chosen for all of us. He is renewing my mind, and he is teaching me, but he seems to be interested in my mind only to the extent that understanding brings me into a greater wholeness of self and relationship with him. He meets me in my prayers, and he soothes my soul there, but he is forever causing my soul to engage my body because that is where my sin lives, and that is where God lays his healing hand. God delights to communicate and spread his goodness through my love and service to others, and nothing feels as wonderful as a moment spent in concert with the Almighty, but God makes use of my physical needs and failures to draw me back to him for a refill because his delight is to know me, and to be known by me, in the context of my ordinary physical world.

When I turn to my body to meet my God, I find a rich and wonderful relationship with an intimate, relational God who offers me the context of his immediate and ongoing embrace — and I find that when I engage life with God right there with me, I tend to pay attention to his love rather than fretting about my failures. I can't think of a more liberating experience than that.

God delights in meeting me in my body, and what he delights in there is not my repentance, or my change, or my usefulness to the kingdom of heaven, but the relationship he experiences with me. My God likes me, enjoys me, and it is the *real* me he meets when he meets me in my body instead of my thoughts, my prayers, or my service, where I tend to offer him mostly stylized, impressively Christian versions of myself. My God delights in his relationship with me, and my relationship with him is the utter definition of who I am.

THE CORE IS RELATIONAL

What I'm about to tell you is good news, but it might not seem like it at first: *Who and what we are is defined by relationship, not by function.* Understanding ourselves outside our merely functional roles is a huge and slippery change in perspective for many of us. At first glance you may not agree that it's huge or slippery at all. You may not think it's even news. It may sound like the same stuff you've been taught and thought all your life.

But if you're like me — if you experience more brokenness than you want to, more shame than you like, more pressure to perform than is good for you, and if you feel you're not very good at being a Christian — then this *is* news.

It just sounds familiar because the language, the now worn and tired words like God and *love* and all of that, have been sucked dry and made into weapons of shame by the disembodied Enlightenment filter we've applied to our faith. After generations of debate and intellectual wrangling, after years of obsessively ignoring Good Friday for the sake of having our faith look Easter-clean to outsiders, life, love, and the God who delights to course through his creation have come to be treated more as "things" than as dynamic relational realities, and in the process they've become boring.

Dear Gnostic-numbed, Docetist-duped friends — it only seems that way.

The very bedrock of existence, the Trinity, is a relationship, not one or three independent beings who happen to work well together. If you want to see the Trinity, don't look to the three parts; look to the relationship between the Father, Son, and Spirit. St. Augustine talked about the Father as the lover, the Son as the beloved, and the Spirit as the searching love that passes between them. Each part is staggeringly glorious, but what is of supreme value and majesty is the way holy glory submits in love and delight, each portion of the relationship in harmonious choreography with the others.

If you want to truly see yourself, look to the relationships that define you. You are best understood not as an entity, but as a part of a relationship (which, by the way, is also why nobody's ever really been able to answer the questions of "who am I" or "why am I here" — they were never meant to be answered by single voices because we don't make sense alone. As my friend Nate Larkin says, "Christianity is a team sport, not an individual event.")

This relational reality is what comes into clear view on Good Friday. This is the core truth that makes "the body of Christ" not a figure of speech or the label for our club, but a living, relational reality. This is how "the two become one," be they husband and wife or the Father and Son who model oneness for all believers. And this small shift, this understanding that sounds so familiar but is so slippery to our usual way of thinking, changes everything.

STORIES OF RELATIONSHIPS AND LIES

When we make room for the concepts of God and love, but don't make room for relationship with the God of love, we quickly become tyrants, slaves, or fools, depending on how we err. I've been all three, and I've been a variety of each of them.

I've become several kinds of tyrant when I've sought to control my sense of value and denied God's insistence that I am acceptable exactly as I am.

I've fallen into various kinds of slavery when I've believed that my voice doesn't matter, and that slavery has left me feeling stuck and unseen by my God.

And I've been at least four flavors of fool when I've tried to play God's role for him and forgotten that God will always be the one pursuing me, and will always do the real work in our relationship.

The more I see about how I've related to God, the more I see the same dynamics played out in my other relationships. My dad, for one. My relationship with my dad is an important case study as I reconsider the ways I've experienced the world. I see how I tend to interact with the version of my dad who lives in my head and in my own confused thinking, instead of interacting honestly with the actual guy. I've put words in his mouth, including words describing who I am and what I'm worth. I've been wrong, and if I'm going to be free, I need to knock it off.

In much the same way, the Church has a tendency to interact with our version of God instead of interacting with the God who loves to make himself known. We've put words in God's mouth, including words describing who we are and what we're worth. We've been wrong, and if we're going to be free, we need to knock it off.

The good news, as I continue to look behind the misconceptions I've had about a God who turns out to really like me, is that ... well ... God really likes me and delights in being with me.

Broken man that I am.

Discussion Questions

1. If you pray for healing, and do not receive healing, what does that make you feel?

2. How do you feel about a God who talks about love, but doesn't heal you?

3. Do you believe, in everyday thoughts, not just Sunday school thoughts, that God is good?

4. Where might your thinking need to change if God is good AND he doesn't heal you?

5. Read Romans 7. What do you think of the idea that your brokenness may not be you, but sin living within you, as a disease within your body (or "members," as Paul says)?

6. *If it were true* that it is no longer you who sins, but sin living within you, how might that truth change the way you experience your failures?

7. Where have you been taught that your sins are a matter of your personal weakness, rather than an aspect of the fall of all creation?

8. Why do you want to sin less?

My grace is sufficient for you,
for my power is made perfect in weakness.
2 CORINTHIANS 12:9

PART II

TYRANTS

CHAPTER 2

THE TRUE BELIEVER:
SCARCITY RUN AMOK

I was a Boy Scout when I was in junior high, living in Seattle. The troop was all about outdoor adventures — weeklong hikes in the summer, several long weekend excursions at different times of year, stuff like that. When you turned fourteen, you were allowed to do the Mt. Rainier weekend, which entailed digging and sleeping in snow caves and being lowered into glacial crevasses for rescue training. It was a great place to be a Boy Scout, and I'm sure that most of my friends from that season of my life have nothing but great memories of the group.

But I was a little chubby, a little spoiled, and more than a little weak when it came to dealing with discomforts, so for me the time was filled with embarrassments and failures that somehow lodged themselves into my view of the world and still show up now and then in the form of goofy thinking and tacit fears.

Many of the fears and the self-perceptions I carry today have a lot to do with the ways I learned to think of and talk to myself during those clumsy years.

The clearest, most convincing glimpse into what I must really be like lodged itself into my thinking during a weekend hiking trip on the coast of Washington when I was twelve. I didn't know it at the time, and frankly didn't even realize it until quite recently, but that single weekend trip shaped the tone of voice I've used on myself ever since. It created my most stubborn filters about how God sees and speaks to me.

FALLING DOWN

For me, the weekend was miserable from the beginning. The first night we camped in the rain, and by morning my sleeping bag was soaked. It was my first experience using any of my camping gear, and I didn't have the physical strength to get the wet bag into the stuff sack quickly enough for my dad, who was already frustrated by the conditions and by my fussy responses to them. I was crying before breakfast.

I was the slowest hiker, often lagging a half mile behind the next slowest people from the troop. I liked looking around, popping kelp, picking up shells, and generally not hiking with purpose. The walking wasn't hard, just boring. A couple times my dad waited for me to hurry me up. I was afraid of him. I didn't want to let him down. But I also remember feeling like the father-son trip was supposed to be about time spent together, not whatever it was that had him hurrying and then waiting to tell me to hurry. I kept expecting him to realize his mistaken priorities like dads on TV do.

Somewhere along the trail I picked up a small, smooth piece of white shell. I remember carrying it in my hand, and lightly rubbing its smoothness against my upper lip. I felt grateful for that bit of comfort — but also felt that the piece of shell was mocking proof of my weirdness. I knew not to show it to my dad. In those hours I learned something to the effect that my treasures would always be weird and silly and the source of frustration to other people.

Later in the day I fell in a stream when my dad, aggravated by my too careful approach, pushed me from behind to hurry me along. I came up spitting water and, as I tried to regain my footing, I slipped again. I knew my dad hadn't meant for me to fall when he pushed me, and we both hurried to get beyond the clumsy situation. He took some stuff from my pack, and one of the other fathers, who'd been a short distance ahead of me and who returned when he'd heard the splashing, took some of my other gear. It was so embarrassing. I was so embarrassing.

Then came the worst part of the hike: about a mile of beach covered in large round rocks, maybe three feet tall. They were usually too close together to walk around them. My dad could step up onto one and down the other side. But for me it was hand, hand, knee, knee, foot, foot, down. It was miserable going. We were the last ones on the beach. The sun had gone down and it was dark.

My dad either hadn't brought a flashlight or for some reason decided to use the one I'd brought — a tiny penlight that his pharmaceutical sales force gave out to physicians as a novelty item. He'd climb over each rock, stop, and shine the light for me — with some sort of advice or comment about each hurdle — and then we'd repeat the process. When we arrived at the camp, the only place to set up our tent was on loose stones, which made for nightmarish sleeping for which I felt responsible.

MEASURING UP

The challenges and failures of the hiking trip were minor, really. Nothing serious happened. But the fact that everything was so ordinary is what made the message I took from the experience so easy to believe. My negative self-talk seemed reasonable. I was weak and thin-skinned. My shortcomings were an embarrassment, a burden on other people. My weakness and my lack of focus were bad. So bad my dad never came on a hike again. He never said he quit hiking with me because I made him miserable, but I saw that I didn't measure up — not even to the most basic standards. I had failed, and to me it seemed as though I didn't have a big enough credit balance with my dad for him to try again.

A significant portion of my adult self is rooted in the grading system of that weekend's failure. The conclusions I reached about myself and about what it means to be grown up made sense in light of that experience. And those beliefs had dried and solidified before I prayed for salvation three years later. So I received Jesus as Lord of the heart and of a life I'd learned to describe elsewhere. And sadly, the Jesus of my evangelical experience sounded a lot like the voices of shame and performance and failure I'd already been practicing. The Jesus I was taught confirmed the snide contempt I'd already come to feel for myself. He'd be a more patient taskmaster, perhaps, but my shame and my perceptions of my weakness were givens that I never thought to ask God to correct or comment on. And for one reason or another, nobody else gave me reason to ask him about those givens either.

Pet Name

When I was in my twenties and decided to throw myself into my faith, pursuing a variety of professional ministry endeavors, I did what the seventh grader in me had come away from that hiking trip thinking was the right way to do things. I stuffed that sleeping bag, no matter how I felt. I walked fast along that beach, urging others to do likewise — after all, the view is the same for hundreds of miles along that stretch of coast. I pushed people, even if my pushing caused them to fall. Then I picked them up and helped carry their load, even if the load wasn't the problem nearly so much as was the pace or my approach to travel. I sure as heck had my flashlight ready, and I was proud of it — all full of answers and advice and rock-by-rock insistencies, or petty revenge when my counsel was not heeded to my liking.

I was still clumsy, and still pretty weak, but I kept pushing. I was not going to be that kid again. I was not going to be rejected for failing at things other people could do. I would have talked about discipline or strength or some word that didn't sound like shame or condemnation, but inside I had the feeling that God had one passive-aggressive but good-natured pet name for me: Dumbass.

In fact, my friend Skinny Robert used to joke with me about it. We'd say things like:

"What kind of fish are you?"

"Bass," with a really deep, dumb sound to it.

"What kind of bass?"

"Dumb."

At one point during my time in Denver, I considered going to Syria as a missionary. Skinny Robert's reply?

"You'd put the Dumbass in Damascus."

I think most fanatics, or "true believers," as they're also called,

43

are motivated by a deep shame and fear that their best efforts will not be enough. They are convinced that the people who *are* acceptable to God — other people, usually heroes or "tremendous men of God" — will all score at or above some vaguely high percentile. They may not be as in touch with descriptions of developmentally delayed sea creatures as Skinny Robert and I were; they likely use big, defensive terms instead. But they put out fear and effort, and they shun the last smooth shell of comfort and cram it away in the far recesses of their hearts. They starve themselves of a reasonable comfort any child would know to expect. Or they steal ghosts of those comforts in the form of irrational addictions elsewhere.

Today I am a year older than my father was the weekend of the hiking trip, and it's easy for me to see what it would have been like for him. Recently I asked my dad about the hiking trip and about my old pet name, Dumbass. I asked him what he thinks God thinks about when looking at him. It was telling to hear his answer.

"You're born this perfect little creature," my dad said, "all potential and clean, and God is so pleased with what he's made. And then he watches us make our choices" — here my dad purses his lips a bit and starts to shake his head slowly back and forth — "and he says, 'You're screwin' it all up, kid.'"

That sounded familiar. I guess it's no surprise that we can teach only the freedoms or prisons we know.

Reprogramming

Two winters ago I'd lost a bunch of weight on the trendy solution that was in fashion at the time, and I decided to celebrate by going hiking by myself. A few people voiced concerns about me doing five hilly miles at 300 pounds, but I was feeling strong, and their concerns turned it into a sort of vision quest for me. I decked myself out in wool and fabric that sounds like zippers when I walk, and I headed into the frozen forest toward the lake.

The hills were steeper than I'd anticipated, and hike in was very hard for me. But I hadn't brought my flashlight, and I wanted to get to the lake before the sun went down, so I had to keep pushing. There were moments when I thought of my dad, and I grinned about the fact that we all seem destined to become our parents. I found myself urging myself forward with the same sorts of tactics I'd learned from him years before and had applied in a variety of ways since. I was stronger than the hill. I was not a wuss. Anybody can hike five miles. I didn't want to have to tell people I'd stopped short, at some unknown location some unknown distance from my objective. I didn't know how much farther I had to go, and the sun was fading, so I just kept marching. I made it to the lake and gathered a bunch of wood for the fire I started before I let myself sit down.

The sky was clear and the sun was fizzling out to the west. It was beautiful. But the night was going to be cold. I will never forget standing beside the fire, pausing as I changed into dry clothing, enjoying the chill, enjoying the thrill of being exposed with no walls around me, just the fire and the sun slipping red behind the far shore of the lake, a gentle breeze blowing my way, chilling my giant naked whiteness.

In my mind, I can return there in an instant.

I did it. I didn't know if I'd be able to make it, but it was no big deal after all. I claim the victory and stand warrior proud before the world to say so.

The dry T-shirt feels so soft slipping onto my shoulders, sliding over my cold stomach. Out of the long underwear, I pull the pants back up. The built-in cloth belt is wet with sweat, but will be okay.

Fresh wool socks. Wool sweater. Hat. I should have brought a second hat because the one I've been wearing is sweaty. Gloves.

Plastic tarp on the ground to keep the moisture away. I lay it on the leeward side of the fire so the heat will carry my direction. The self-inflating pad. The sleeping bag. I put the wet clothing over a log beside the fire in hopes of having them dry before I pack them back up tomorrow. I light a cigar and call home on the cell phone. I get the machine and leave a message telling my wife that I survived the hike in, and that I'm turning the phone off because the battery's low.

I'm here. I made it. Good job. I'm warming back up. The fire's good. Should have plenty of wood to keep the fire going until well after I fall asleep, with enough to warm up again in the morning when I crawl out of the sleeping bag. I sit on the bag in my stocking feet and smoke and watch the sunset. Yep. Here I am. Well done. I'll probably be sore tomorrow, but there won't be any hurry, so I'll be able to enjoy the walk back out. For now I'll just sit and enjoy the evening.

For a really, really long time. It's only six o'clock. Hadn't thought about the whole early-sunset-in-winter thing. Didn't bring a book. Didn't bring a journal. Don't want to walk around. No way I'd be able to fall asleep yet. Not for at least another three hours. That's a long time to just sit on my sleeping bag doing nothing. But it doesn't have to be, I guess. This is a sort of vision quest. A kind of claim to life. A refusal to give in to death quite yet. I open myself up to God. I invite him to be with me. I thank him for the day, for this place, for this moment and the wink of sunset still hanging in the sky, twinkling in stars directly above me now. It looks like some clouds are coming, which would be good for keeping the night from getting too frigid.

I'm going to die tonight. The thought pierces my brain. I'm going to die. It feels like a premonition. It feels like it could be God telling me this. Fear shoots through me. Not fair. Not now, not now that I'm on the right track. Don't punish me for the sins I'm trying to leave behind. Not fair. I don't want to die tonight.

I'm going to die tonight. The thought sits beside me and patiently drums its fingernails on the log beside the fire. *Not right-right now, but very soon. Certainly before dawn. Certainly before dawn.* God doesn't talk like this. How do I know how God talks? How do I know how he'd tell me I was going to die? *I'm going to die tonight. Certainly before dawn.*

I deserve it too. I've had this coming. And it's been a long time coming. And on top of everything else lousy and selfish about my death, it's going to require either a boat rental or a ten-mile round trip hike for people to haul my huge carcass from this place. My wife will drive down to Bloomington with my parents. She and my mom will cry the whole way, and Dad will be stern and efficient, torn up inside but taking care of the situation. I'll certainly be dead before dawn, and I did this to myself. What a dumbass.

I don't call you Dumbass.

It was almost audible.

I don't call you Dumbass.

That was God. The other thoughts were imposters. I know God's voice. He doesn't call me Dumbass. That is not his pet name for me. It's not a cute thing. It's not funny. It's not true. It's simply a non-fit on reality. Stop it.

No more.

He doesn't call me Dumbass. I'm not to call myself Dumbass. I'm not to agree with others who do. God does not call me Dumbass, so the word has nothing to do with me. It is by no means certain that I will die tonight. My life or death are not the point, nor are they mine to seek to insure. They are merely mine to embrace and to enjoy and to grasp firmly for the sake of offering them back to God. I am not a dumbass. God does not call me Dumbass.

I sit with this. I wait for more. I pray. I ask for more. It's only 6:15. I have hours available for miracles. But God has said his piece and has staked his claim, and all I hear is the water lapping against the rocky lakeshore. A thought pokes at me. *You're going to die tonight.*

"I don't think so," I say aloud to the spirit beside me.

LONG NIGHT

The fire smells good. I wash an energy bar down with a bottle of water and throw the trash into the fire. I slip into my untied boots and walk a few feet to pee. It's 9:30 and I think I can fall asleep now. I shake the boots off and wiggle into the open sleeping bag, which slides on the plastic sheet beneath it so I end up slipping downhill a bit and look like I could be spooning with the log. There's a gap beneath the log where the orange firelight shines through. I grab the zipper tab by my knees and begin to close up the sleeping bag I've had for years. I can't zip it past my stomach. I'm too fat to close the sleeping bag over my upper body.

The demon of hatred perks up and grins.

I can still draw the hood portion of the bag around my head and close the Velcro at the neck. I'll be fine. I make the mental shift from bed comfort standards to ground comfort and, after a few adjustments, I sputter to sleep.

For about an hour.

The wind is picking up and it looks like the clouds may carry rain. Or snow. Or sleet. Sleet would totally suck. I'm shivering. I put on the rest of the clothes. My legs feel fine, so I put the long underwear around my neck like a scarf. I duck my face into them a little to block the cold. The smell answers a question I'd had earlier about whether or not I should wear regular underwear under the long underwear. But I don't care. This is getting serious. It was thirty degrees out when I left the car in the middle of the afternoon — it must be in the teens now. I have at least seven or eight hours until it'll be light enough to hike out, and I don't have a flashlight. I'll wake up in a little while and make adjustments if I have to.

I have to. The demon dances around me, joyfully doing what it can to scare me and make me use the *D* word. I pile some more wood on the fire. I hang the other clear plastic tarp between two trees behind me to create a wind block.

I'm very tired.

An hour later I pull my boots back on and head into the forest to find more wood. I haven't burned everything I gathered before, but there's no way I have enough to make it through the night, and it seems like a bad idea to wait until I'm out before I gather more. I can't see a thing. I pull my keys from my pocket and use the little LED light-up-your-keyhole light to pick my way over the stream and to the place where I saw some wood before. I'm scared, but it's also an adventure. I know it's only as big an emergency as I let it become.

"Okay, so I'm not a dumbass. Does that mean this isn't stupid?" I ask God. I feel him grin.

I load the fire up some more, kick my boots off, and cram myself into the bag as well as I can. Somewhere along the hike or somewhere during the evening, Queen's "Bohemian Rhapsody" got stuck in my head, and it's driving me nuts.

"Galileo Galileo. Figaro. Magnifico-o-o-o-o."

An hour later I'm up again, breaking out the emergency blanket. What a scam those things are. I was expecting some NASA superstar, super warm great thing. No. It's just a freakin' reflective candy wrapper. More wood on the fire. Another hour of sleep.

"I'm just a poor boy from a poor family …"

By three o'clock I'm up for good. I tie the reflective emergency blanket around my neck like a cape, put the sleeping bag on top of that, and stand in the night beside my fire trying to stop thinking, "Any way the wind blows … nothing really matters … to me." Freddie Mercury can bite me.

I gather more wood and burn it. I burn the log that I'd been spooning before. I watch the purples deep in the fire. The spirit that had been whispering to me before reclines in the shadows of a tree off to my right, glaring at me in frustration. God said I win. I'm just waiting, packing up and staying warm on this beach, getting ready for the dawn I already know is mine. God speaks life. It's my task to endure the night and to pack up in the morning and get moving.

It's true that the darkest hour is just before dawn. I'm moving as soon as there's light enough to do so. I'm sore and tired and defiant — and still scared. I feel disoriented. I know that my sense of drama about the night and what I'd heard from God are going to fade as soon as I hit the warmth and lamplight of my regular world. It's usually that way, I guess.

The sun filters through bare trees along the ridge and sparkles on frost and ice. I feel guilty about burning the logs someone else dragged into place around the fire. I shouldn't have burned the plastic water bottles. That was bad for the environment. I used up all of the fire starter paste — it was a big tube too — and I dropped that trash into the fire.

Crunching my way through the woods, I feel as though I have no right to be here. The fatigue and the dramatic night have me thinking strange thoughts. Suddenly I find myself very much afraid of being gored by a deer like I'd seen on home video shows on television — as though deer are lurking behind trees, stalking me, waiting to ambush me. Or drop down on me from tree branches with camouflage ninja bandanas around their antlered foreheads.

It had been a long night with too little sleep. I feel like a three-hundred-pound guy who'd been lucky to live through one night on his own just outside of town.

I feel heavier than that as I trudge up the hills, hearing nothing but my wheezing breathing and the punching sound my boots make on the hard dirt.

I don't want to keep going. I want to quit. I feel the old, childish panic welling up — the panic that comes from feeling like the challenge is too much. The one that makes the kid in me want to lie down and cry, that thinks the football coach is being too mean or that Dad shouldn't make me edge and weed the yard after mowing it. A childish panic, but a real one. On the way to the lake, I'd been talking myself into being tough guy optimistic about the hike. Now it just feels hard.

Hey, it's okay. You can do this. Stop for ten seconds, then walk to that tree up there. Then stop and turn around and look at what you've done. You can do it. It's okay.

And I do. And I tell myself "good job." And I do it again. And again. And again. And during the course of the five miles, a stronger and more able self comes gently beside the boy self and takes care of him. I come alongside myself. I become a little bit more whole. *Good job, Sweetheart,* I say.

When you've spent years calling yourself Dumbass, and have filtered life and even God through the sort of worldview that gives rise to that sort of pet name, something big happens when the name Sweetheart arrives on the scene.

Soon I am weeping, letting go, finally ready to be done with one of the worst things, one of the worst days.

Battle of the True Believer

It happened one afternoon when I was a junior and my brother was a freshman in high school. He'd dropped football the year before — to the great chagrin of our father — and had started playing the drums instead, which to me seemed to result in a new layer of distance between my dad and the brother who'd always been the one ... the one Mom watched out for most.

I'd stuck with football. I wasn't good, and I wasn't a starter. Practices were humiliating to me, and if we'd been at a larger high school I wouldn't have played at all. But I didn't have the courage to stand up to my father — or more accurately to the impressions of him that I trusted more than the realities of him. I had no idea how to quit. So I kept going, slave to the voices of ridicule in reality and in the diatribes of my mind.

I don't remember what triggered the moment between my brother and me. We were both in the kitchen. I probably wanted some food that he had and said something about it being mine. He probably said something about how not everything was for me, or something about my being a jock, or some other antagonism. I don't recall.

I do remember pushing him. I remember challenging him, getting in his face. I remember punching him in the arm. I remember the things I said to him. Things about how he should fight back, how he should hit me. How he should stand up for himself. About how Dad thought he was weak. How my brother's refusal to stand up for himself was a huge part of the reason Dad treated him the way he did. A huge reason why Dad didn't love him.

Didn't love him.

He began to cry, but he wouldn't give in to the tears. His eyes went red and his face took on that shocked expression a person gets when the tips of their toes are searching for the bottom of the pool. He looked like he couldn't tell just how horrible the things I was saying were going to be for him, how far down he would be pushed. He looked like I was giving voice to all of his worst fears and darkest suspicions.

And the look on his face made me start to cry. It brought me too close to the fears of my own savage doubts. I hated him for quitting football, for making obvious the conditionality of our father's attention. I hated how tenuous that made my own security. I was not good at football. I was not good at anything in particular. I could be shut out too. My brother's experiences showed me what I would know if I failed. If I quit.

I pushed him and I yelled at him to fight back.

"Hit me!"

And he would not. He backed into the corner of the counters and slumped to the floor as I stood over him.

"Hit me!" I shrieked, desperate. "If you hit me, Dad will love you!"

He would not. He crawled past me and raced to his bedroom with me on his heels. He locked the door and I banged on it, sobbing in an insane rage. Inside, he screamed that he hated me ... hated me ... hated me.

By dinner, things were back to normal. The cycle of emotions was familiar enough to both of us. The monstrosity of our sense of them was so overwhelming that neither of us ever said a word about it again.

That was the day the bully won out in my heart, the bully that was afraid of being inadequate, of being found out. The bully that called me Dumbass. The bully that found such a home in the role of true believer. Between that day and the morning of my laboring from the lake to the car I had never spoken a kind word to myself. I had moved between false cruelty and false weakness, either in the form of obviously foolish optimism or falsely plaintive wallowing. The hills and cold of my life had been nothing but misery for me. I had permitted myself no encouragement. There had been only the bully standing over me, or me as the bully … standing in a rage above my cowering self.

But during that hike in the woods back to my car, the bully called me Sweetheart. Something changed. As I drive back to Indianapolis and my wife, that is all I can think about, shivering in my sweat-soaked 4-X T-shirt.

I am still terrified about the other hills and the cold of life I feel. I don't want to dredge this up. I don't want to climb. I want to lie down and cry. But I know what is being said within me, for the first time in almost twenty years.

Oh, Sweetheart. You can do this. It will be okay.

DISCUSSION QUESTIONS

1. Think about the piece of smooth seashell Pete rubbed on his lip during the hike with his father. Where did you find comforts as a child? Where do you find comforts now? How do you feel about those comforts and what they say about you?

2. What pet name or descriptive phrase do you *live as though* God has for you? How did that description get planted into your heart?

3. How do you feel about that description?

4. How has that description helped you in your life?

5. How has that description worked against you?

6. How have your experiences with Christianity reinforced that name?

7. What name would you most love to hear God use to draw you to him?

CHAPTER 3

THE RICH MAN:
WHAT THE GOOD SEAT DOES TO A SOUL

The messages from the childhood of my friend Dan were like my own, but louder, and he believed them more completely. Twisted and cruel though these beliefs are, they've led him to remarkable success. The curse of the rich man is that the comforts brought to him by his success shame him with the question: "Who are you to complain?" Comfort and success stifle a rich man with shame and teach him that he must always see himself, and his pain, as compared to what he sees in others. The admission of pain is the only luxury a rich man cannot afford.

A stifled rich man is a dangerous brother, a fiercely tyrannical believer, and he needs a special sort of love if he's to be restored.

Driven to Succeed

Dan comes from a divorced family, was small for his age, and probably spent time alone when he would have benefited from socialization. There are stories of cruelty at home and from peers, and because he was so alone as a child, there was nobody to help Dan figure out what to make of his experiences. The voices of shame and inadequacy in his world were thorough, and where I've tended to respond to condemnation by risking more or by giving in to the tears, Dan learned at a young age that it would be better for him to pull any sort of vulnerability into his shell.

He ran a painting company when he was in high school and made a good chunk of cash while his classmates were doing more ordinary teen things. He was different, and the difference made him feel good — safe, maybe. In control, at least. He started a record company with a friend while he was in college. The two wore ties to the bars and other concert venues to remind themselves and their clients that they were businessmen and that the production and assorted music services they offered were merely aspects of the business. Years of serious hard work and way-beyond-average risks built the company. Its sale meant that Dan had achieved the financial ability to retire at the age of thirty.

He's also a sky diver.

And an accomplished kayaker.

And an award-winning songwriter.

Last year he became fluent in Spanish so he could communicate better with some of the employees at one of the several companies in which he has ownership stakes.

There is a darkroom in his basement.

He builds his external attributes, his claims to fame, the descriptions other people can use to explain him. But very few people are allowed in to see the Dan behind the accomplishments. That person is still the same kid who learned long ago to protect himself. And that kid is a lot like a wild animal — the sort that doesn't know how to make eye contact without seeing the eye contact as a dare, a challenge to combat.

It's that combination, that pairing of aggression and self-expression through external accomplishment, that keeps Dan isolated. That, and the fact that no matter what interesting things Dan adds to his list of activities, he is still usually seen mostly for his money.

People don't ask him to volunteer — they ask him to join their board.

Ministry leaders make clumsy, awkward jokes about having him pick up the tab for lunch or how, if they had known he was going to pick up the tab, they would have scheduled a supersonic flight to Paris for really good croissants "or however you say that word."

Dan doesn't know how to share who he really is; that was drummed out of him as a child. People who would like to know him as a person eventually give up trying to hack through the external descriptions Dan uses as the camouflage that keeps him from being seen as just another guy. He complains of feeling alone, but he can't quite make himself risk what he would need to risk to be truly seen … by people who may or may not like what they discover. So Dan is left wandering in a series of relationships that interact with his external self, his hobbies, his business sense, his energy, his money — but not with him.

People don't call a rich man a rich man because he has money. A rich man is a rich man because most of the time that's all we know to say about him.

Driven to Drive

Dan is like many wealthy people. He doesn't drive a great car, doesn't live in a giant house, and doesn't do anything extravagant, really. Except that, like many wealthy people, when Dan engages, he engages with a passion and potency that is stunningly fierce and productive.

It's way too close to the core for Dan to agree, but I think his passion comes from a deep response to shame. He doesn't have many gears — pretty much just ON and OFF. Dan cannot accept failure, from himself or from people near him. And that makes Dan a real handful in relationships. The word is codependent. If there's a horse and white hat to be found, Dan's there, riding hard and charging forward. And man, when Dan's on that horse, the horse sure seems like a high one.

This, though, seems to be the prerogative of the rich man in much of our world. He's achieved success, so he's allowed to run roughshod where he chooses. That's what drives businesses to success, and it's also the price a great many churches and nonprofit organizations pay for the help or the cash of their rich men.

It's too bad that it only makes things worse for people like my friend.

The biggest struggle in most of Dan's life is that his ON and OFF gears mean that he comes on too strong with his help or his engagement. Dan has enough money that a serious effort from him would swamp most local ministries, just as it often swamps his relationships. Where he's concerned, we talk a lot about not "strapping rockets to the Kitty Hawk."

Four years ago Dan and I decided he'd help me lose some weight and get into better shape. At the time we didn't understand that we were both driven by adequacy issues, and it didn't go well. He took two gallon milk jugs, wrote my name on the sides of them, and filled them with water. He carried the jugs on his runs, as though he was carrying some of my burden, and he prayed for me as he ran and drank. He showed me the significant chafing that developed where his arms rubbed against his ribs. Another time he decided to walk instead of run at the high school track, the way I have to walk instead of run, and the burden and the boredom of it got to him. He ended up on his knees on the track, crying for me, with strangers having to swerve around him. He told me about this.

How do you say thank you for that sort of gesture? I mean, I was doing the walking and I was dieting, but in some ways he was more invested in the process than I was. Dan's drive was greater than my own, so before long I severed the connection between us out of shame. Rockets on the Kitty Hawk, and the pain of failure and rejection for him — when what he'd intended was to love the only way he knew how.

It's not just diet stuff, either. Dan was the driver with his partner at the record label and a series of other joint business ventures over the course of about fifteen years. They experienced success together, with Dan's pushing fueled to unhealthy intensity by his success-wrapped fears of inadequacy. Eventually the partner had had enough. They'd earned plenty of money, and Dan's partner was no longer interested in being pushed to be a super achiever. The partnership, and the deeper parts of the friendship, eventually blew up. That much time, and that many narrow places, and that many choices to push forward together. The breakup has not been an easy change for either man, and for Dan it has been more than a little disorienting.

Dan was doing the best he knew to do. He never meant for things to get sideways like they did. He knows there is something broken in him (just like there is something broken in fat guys who don't get skinny), but he doesn't know what to do about it. And that makes the shame even more daunting and even cunning to a guy like Dan.

DRIVEN BY DUTY

Like many self-made affluent people, Dan has a sense of moral obligation that goes beyond what many other people feel. Something inspired by his privileged position in society. The French call it *noblesse oblige*, nobility obliges, in reference to the duty stronger members of society have to weaker members. Dan has a powerful sense of duty to be his brother's keeper. That duty creates moments of confusion for Dan and other people in his world because his sense of duty is about Dan, and about what is right for him, and not about what other people may understand. What's more, when a weaker brother is blessed by a stronger brother, the weaker brother usually has little sense of what it truly costs the stronger brother, and that adds an additional twist and challenge to Dan's burden as a rich man.

For example, Dan was the mostly hands-off part owner of a small sailing club and marina with another, different partner. That man had convinced his mother-in-law to put her family's large home, which had been built by her grandfather a hundred years earlier, up as collateral on the business loan. When the marina failed due to subpar management, the man's mother-in-law lost the estate in the bankruptcy.

What to do, if you're the rich man? The question was not what the law, or any social rule, demanded of Dan. The question facing Dan was "what's the right thing to do?"

He bought the estate and gave it back to the family.

And if you're the man whose marina failed, whose wife's elderly mother lost the family estate because of you, and someone buys it back for her to cover your failure, how do you even begin to express your gratitude? What do you say to Dan? How do you view his generosity? What do you owe him? Do you owe him anything? How much must it hurt to feel that wholly unable to return the favor? How can the relationship possibly go forward from there?

Rockets on the Kitty Hawk. The gift totally shreds the recipient — the rockets tear the wings right off.

If you're Dan, and you've done the right thing because it was the right thing, not because you owed the man anything, what do you say next? After your failed partner's fumbled thank-you. How do you respond when the gratitude feels weak or indolent, when it has a vibe that sounds a lot like, "The fact that you were *able* to help must mean that it wasn't all *that* hard a thing for you to do." What do you do when the man doesn't offer repayment, in full or in part, and doesn't seem to be as dedicated to the same sort of "right" as you are? How much must that hurt, to feel that clumsy and that weird and that impossible to thank adequately? What do you say about doing the right thing when the right thing destroys the relationship?

When I think of Dan, I often think of Moses killing the Egyptian in defense of a Jewish slave, and how the other Jewish slaves later ask who the heck Moses thinks he is. Having the power to do the right thing, even doing the right thing, doesn't guarantee you'll be seen as a hero. In fact, life usually goes the other way. This is a core struggle in the lives of rich men.

How does a rich man who is driven by his determination to not be vulnerable, who is succeeding at keeping himself from criticism, who is alone and starving inside, ever come to experience the moment of knowing himself as Sweetheart?

In the book of James, the advice is not to give the good seat to the rich man. It has to do with not seeing the rich man for his money instead of his personhood.

My brothers and sisters, believers in our glorious Lord Jesus Christ must not show favoritism. Suppose someone comes into your meeting wearing a gold ring and fine clothes, and a poor person in filthy old clothes also comes in. If you show special attention to the one wearing fine clothes and say, "Here's a good seat for you," but say to the one who is poor, "You stand there" or "Sit on the floor by my feet," have you not discriminated among yourselves and become judges with evil thoughts?

JAMES 2:1 – 4

What I want to know is why, in a time when there was no economic, social, or political gain to be had in gathering with the Christians, would a rich man even have any interest in being at the meeting in the first place?

DRIVEN TO THE CROSS

All I can come up with is that the pain in the rich man's world drove him to be there. Money and power have no ability to cure the effects of the fall, and the rich man — and Dan — know it. When I give up my seat to the rich man, the gesture is meant to communicate, "Here, you're important. You take this space of honor"; but what I'm really saying is, "Your world is fine. Who are you to complain?" And when I say that, I deny him permission to need the comfort of the Cross.

When I give my seat to the rich man, I tell him his pain is offensive to me because all I see are the comforts of his world. I don't see Dan as an ordinary guy who loves in clumsy ways, who is scarred by the fat people who reject his encouragement, by partners who don't want to be his partners anymore, or by the men he rescues who can no longer look him in the eye.

If he's especially brave, or utterly broken, he will fight through my curse. But more often, and until the damage gets bad enough, he will fall for the temptation that allows him to feel important, even in ministry settings where he's supposedly defined by his utter need for the Cross. That's a messed-up situation, and Christ is rejected in it.

We all have areas of our lives where we are the rich man. Wherever we say, "Who am I to complain?" that's where we accept the curse of the rich man, where we reject the love of Jesus, and where we choose the lie of the false comfort we find in whatever fleeting idol offers us a little shelter.

I'm not encouraging complaining here, by the way. What I am encouraging is the admission of pain, and a confession that our physical, academic, professional, or role-playing comforts are hopelessly unable to make us whole. The phrase "Who am I to complain?" is not really about refusing to complain. It's about denying pain and, ultimately, it teaches us to reject the embrace of God that is ours at the foot of the Cross. The longer we deny pain, and the more we pressurize it — by not admitting its existence until we're at the very ends of our ropes — the more we will slip into judgmental thinking, bitterness of character, and resentment about the lives we've been given.

Resentment is born from the curse of the rich man. So is anger. Fear. Biting humor. Sexism. Racism. They all come because we feel the pain and dissatisfaction of our clumsy attempts to love and the inadequate gratitude we receive from others. And then we don't take our pain seriously enough to let ourselves admit our need for the love that fits us properly, that fills us well, that overflows freely and with honor. We *do* loving acts instead of *being* loving. The curse of the rich man hurts, and it starves us in isolation, until something breaks or until someone invites us to simply be a part of the collection of broken people who are powerless without a God who will indwell, clean house, and change us from the inside out.

Driven to Light

In September 2006, a friend invited me to visit Egypt with him. He wanted me to meet some of his friends in the international sports ministry world. We spent most of a week at a beautiful oasis resort about halfway between Cairo and Alexandria, developing friendships with people from all around the Middle East and North Africa.

I know it sounds like hocus-pocus, but from the first day, I felt as though God was pointing my attention to a young man named Steven. He was from the Nubian mountains of Sudan, athletic, charismatic, with maybe the darkest skin I've ever seen. In my memory he's also wearing a pale blue golf shirt. We shared a couple of meals together with other friends, laughing and working hard to bridge the language gap.

On the fourth day in the desert oasis, in a gazebo amid the young ficus trees, sipping something like mango smoothies, God showed me why he'd wanted me to spend some time with Steven.

I asked Steven about his life. He was born in a remote area, though now he lives in the capital city, Khartoum. He has lost a lot of family members — he doesn't know how many for certain — in the genocide in Sudan's Darfur region. We didn't get into many details, in large part because the language barrier was significant enough that we couldn't discuss delicate things with the delicacy they deserved, but also because I felt ashamed of how little help we in the rest of the world have offered his people. For his part, he said that it was hard for him not to hate me because of my skin color. He said that most of the people who are killing his people have light skin too.

Steven has learned to linger in Good Friday. His world leaves him few other places to find comfort, or forgiveness for the injustices that surround him. He repeatedly directed the conversation toward the Cross when we drifted into too much detail about life in Darfur.

After a while, he asked about me.

What to say?

I wrote a book and am hoping it does well enough that my wife will forgive me for how little money I earned while I was writing it?

Tell him about the huge property tax increases in Indianapolis?

Complain about how my dad pushed me into a stream when I was twelve, and how I used to call myself Dumbass?

What came out was a story about how I felt during the flight from the States to Egypt. I told him I'd purchased a second seat because I didn't want to feel the shame of being the fat guy next to a stranger. I told him about the Frenchman who yelled at me when I bumped his elbow as I made my way to the airplane restroom, and how I couldn't have avoided bumping his elbow. I talked about the way people looked at me as my friend and I made our way through the concourse in Frankfurt to meet our connecting flight. I told him how my wife hasn't wanted to have children with me because she says I'm a "bad risk" because of my weight, and she doesn't want to be a single mother when I widow her. I told Steven about shame.

And I felt shame telling him all of it.

Who am I to complain?

Who am I to follow stories of genocide with my own tale of simple foolish gluttony?

But there in the Egyptian oasis in the gazebo beside the ficus trees over a plastic cup of mango smoothie, Steven cried for me.

He knew there was room for me at the foot of the Cross. His tears showed me that Jesus does not care what brings me to him, so long as I arrive.

The cure for my rich man's curse turned out to be the tears of a Sudanese genocide survivor.

That is why the rich man comes to church, because eventually the rich man will meet a Steven. And once Steven says the rich man has a right to cling to the Cross, the rich man will never let go.

That is why we don't give him the good seat.

Discussion Questions

1. How do you "manage" people's impressions of you to protect yourself from their cheap shots?

2. How do people in your life tend to misunderstand you or pigeonhole you?

3. What benefits do you gain from the way people misunderstand or pigeonhole you?

4. How have other people been hurt by the roles you play?

5. How have you been hurt by the roles you play?

6. Where do you see The Rich Man's curse of "who am I to complain?" in your world?

7. What is the most "spoiled brat" pain in your world that you'd want God to address?

8. Do you *live as though* you believe some of your pain is too petty to bother God about? Why? Where did that belief come from?

CHAPTER 4

The Beggar:
Bargaining for Mercy

A genius is anyone whose IQ is over 130. Forrest Gump's IQ was about 80. My friend Vince had an IQ of 54. Vince experienced a lifetime of frustration and pain because he was, technically, retarded. He also, because of the added dynamic of not quite looking retarded, lived without the visual cue, the safety net of protocol, that protects many disabled people. Vince experienced every instance when someone suddenly realized that he was retarded and raised the emotional limousine window between them. He was isolated and rejected, and he saw it happen over and over again.

Vince's father was not a kind man, and he was embarrassed about Vince's limitations. They spoke on the phone often enough, but their face-to-face interactions were heart wrenching. I frequently saw the father slap the son lightly on the head, and maybe that was all that ever happened; but to me it looked like the father wanted to be able to swing harder, to lash out against the brain that had cost so many fatherly dreams, so many caustic decisions, and so many dollars in different programs and care. Vince knew real pain, and he knew it because he was retarded.

It's no surprise that he hated the word. *Retarded* stood for the limitations he felt and must have seemed like the cause of all his pain. Somewhere in grade school, the rest of us learn not to use the word. We all know to say things like "special needs," or "developmentally delayed," or whatever other polite skirting term makes sense in the moment. Vince spent his life braced for the word, and when it came — pointed at him — it devastated him.

THE RETARDED MAN'S REBUTTAL

Part of my job as residential counselor for Vince included taking him to the doctor from time to time. The three of us would meet, I would step out of the room during the examination, and then I would return for the report from the physician.

One time the doctor used the clinical term *retarded* about Vince, and it nailed Vince. In the car on the way home, Vince pressed himself into the corner where the seat met the door, clearly wanting to be as small as he could be. I tried to explain to him that the doctor hadn't meant to be cruel. I tried to explain that we're all just people, and that we all have different strengths and weaknesses, that we're all strong and weak, just to varying degrees in different aspects of our worlds. Nothing seemed to help. For twenty minutes — and twenty minutes is a long time to experience the sort of intensity Vince was experiencing — he stayed small and silent, scrunched in the corner.

And then he found a defense and comfort for himself that followed a line of reasoning that's been adopted to devastating effect in the world. He sat up a little, centered himself in his seat, and looked at me with a mixture of hopefulness and defiance.

"I may be retarded, but at least I'm not some freak drooling in a wheelchair."

I was stunned. I mean, what obnoxious ingratitude! What monstrous cruelty and blindness of self! Didn't he see that he was practicing exactly the same cruelty that had wounded him?

Yeah, he'd known pain of all sorts because of his situation, but his limitations were also the very reason he'd received so much help and so much slack from people over the years. When you're the beggar, you can't talk smack. Everybody knows that.

At least he wasn't some freak drooling in a wheelchair?

I was angry. Vince was missing the point. What a jerk.

And then the moment turned like a mirror on me. I do the same thing all the time. I compromise with the accusation and then I work like heck to sidestep it and let the condemnation clobber somebody else.

"At least I'm not . . ."

The slogan of beggars everywhere. And it is everywhere. You'll hear it if you listen for it.

"I may be a lousy mom, but at least I'm not abusive."

"I may be a workaholic, but at least I'm not an adulterer."

"I may be a thief, but at least I'm not a rapist."

"I may be a rapist, but at least I'm not a murderer."

"I may be a murderer, but at least I'm not a child predator."

"I may be a predator, but at least I'm not . . ."

I don't know what comes next.

"I may be fat, but at least I'm not like one of those four-hundred-pound freaks they show on TV."

"Step on the scale please, Mr. Gall. Good. That's four-oh-four. Thank you."

Crap.

What do I say to the Vinces of the world who aren't able to find a solid, rational response to the voices of accusation and condemnation in their lives the way I can? Better yet, what the heck is the solid, rational response I need for myself? How do I respond to breaking the four-hundred-pound barrier? Revise my "at least I'm not" statement up to five hundred pounds?

Frankly, most of the time, that's exactly what happens.

But the condemnation and accusations don't stop chasing me just because I acquiesce, do they? And as soon as I complete my "at least I'm not" sentence, it's almost as if I've spoken permission to go that far, as though the really bad news, the news that will force some radical admission or change in behavior, has been snooze-barred to a new threshold.

Who Am I?

"At least I'm not ..." is the accursed slogan of the beggar.

"Who am I to complain?" is the accursed slogan of the rich man.

And they're two sides of the same coin, because as soon as you accept one, you're chased down by the other.

At least Vince wasn't a freak drooling in a wheelchair. Therefore, who is Vince to complain about the pain in his world?

At least I don't weigh 500 pounds. Therefore, who am I to complain about the pain and shame and lack of control that got me to 404?

We — at least Vince and I — tend to end up defining ourselves in the negative. "At least I'm not" and "Who am I to" are both statements of negation instead of the affirmative that would be "I am ..."

Vince is retarded.

I do weigh 404 pounds.

It's not how we'd like it, but at least that's something to work with. At least then we show up and exist on the radar, instead of only knowing ourselves by where we do not show up. And frankly, any expression of affirmative existence is a good thing.

Light exists. Darkness is merely the absence of light and it does not exist in and of itself.

Heat exists. Coldness is merely the absence of heat and it does not exist in and of itself.

Love exists. Numb isolation is merely the absence of love and it does not exist in and of itself.

Retardation exists.

Addiction exists.

Vince exists.

I exist.

It's hard to admit the affirmative truths about our existence, whether it's stuff we like or stuff we don't like.

It's hard to admit these truths in the secular world because the secular world can offer no comfort or meaning profound enough to make the truth worth admitting. If there is no God, admitting we exist is an admission unto despair.

Admitting the truth in the Christian world is rough because as soon as you show up in the affirmative, herds of people challenge you with "Who are you to complain?" Or they receive your presence as a sort of condemnation that causes them to jump-start their own well-I-may-be ... but-at-least-I'm-not ... routine. Somewhere along the way we decided admitting the truth is anti-social behavior, and we agreed to stop seeming so ... *human* all the time. I know there was a memo about it — it came from Colorado Springs, or Grand

Rapids, or Orlando, or Franklin, Tennessee ... I think. Maybe Rome, by way of Germany. Who knows.

My friend, I'm sorry that I've trusted the language of negation and hiding more than I've trusted the affirmations of my Maker, and that I've thought so little of you that I've assumed you'd be unwilling to make room for my existence. I've made the world less real because of my fears and my own smallness. I've made the world scarier and meaner for people like Vince. I've taught him horrible ways to cope with the fright that is the inauguration of self in the kingdom — the part where we see ourselves in matter-of-fact terms, admit our status as contingent, fallen beings, and begin to live from the truth that...

We exist, we are loved, and we should be.

DISCUSSION QUESTIONS

1. For Vince, the worst thing anybody could call him was *retarded*. What is the worst, most terrifying thing a person could call you?

2. Vince's word, *retarded*, was terrifying because it was true, and he couldn't change it, and he wasn't sure what the word ultimately meant about him. How is your "worst word" similar?

3. The Beggar's Curse, "at least I'm not," is one way for people to negotiate with the hard truths in their worlds. How do you describe the difference between interacting with hard but true matters of fact, like being retarded or weighing 404 pounds, and interacting with the meanings we attach to those matters of fact? For example, the hard fact may be "I weigh 404 pounds," but the meaning may be "I am embarrassing," or "I am weak," or "I should be ashamed of myself," or "I cannot be credible because of this fact about me."

4. Where are your "at least I'm not" arguments taking you?

CHAPTER 5

THE CYNIC:
HYPERBOLE IS ALWAYS STUPID

"Keep coming back."

It's what other people in the recovery programs say to you when you're new, when you're just barely hanging on, or when you obviously haven't given up control of your life to God. The other people in the program say it as encouragement, of course, but it's also a way for them to let go of you so you don't drag them down. There is always a macabre sort of fascination with despair that, like the gripping view of a car wreck, draws people in and distracts them from where they want to go.

"Keep coming back."

The program works. The truth that's being spoken is clear and transformative, but it can penetrate only so far, so quickly, through the filters of our addictions and preconceptions. I was a serious follower of Jesus for twenty years before I understood that he doesn't call me Dumbass. Sometimes the most important thing is that you don't give up, and sometimes all you can say to the person with the thick filters is, "Keep coming back."

So long as you're still coming back — to group, to church, to God, and ultimately to the brokenness, unwilling to give up quite yet — you're not a cynic. You may be a doubter or a prophet or a reformer, or you may simply be in a bad fit in one setting or another; but doubt and change and searching for a good fit are all good things. The cynic is the person who hears the invitation to come back and responds with "Yeah, whatever." In the world of recovery programs, cynics die.

In the world outside recovery programs — and since all of life is recovery, there isn't really a world outside of recovery — cynics die.

POWERLESSNESS = CHOICE

There's a guy in my recovery program — really he could be anybody there — whose story terrifies me. He's a black guy named William, about fifty years old, who must weigh six hundred pounds. The part about him being black is relevant because he's a chemist who comes from a family of modest means, and he carries not only the weight of his addiction, but the burden of his family's pride in sense of success. I've known people like William before — amazingly intelligent, with a long history of winning praise and success by using their minds. He's talked enough about his family that I know it was very important to them that William succeed in school and in his professional life. In many ways, he's been set up as their champion, the one who will make them all proud. In many ways, that's been good for William. But in other ways it's clear that somewhere along the line, something in him was broken by the demands of his family. William's emotions terrify him, and he's unable to let himself trust God even though he's often nearly suicidal — literally. He knows that whatever he's doing isn't working.

Last Saturday, William told us he'd received "a death sentence" from his doctor. The doctor said William needs to lose three hundred pounds or he will die, and that his only option is bariatric surgery. William cried as he talked about it. He is terrified. He is ashamed of what he has done to himself. I get that.

But here's the thing: it's not a death sentence if William allows himself to get help. It's a painful and humiliating and scary prospect, certainly, but it is only a death sentence for the cynic who cannot yield and who will not admit defeat. It's not even defeat, really. It's putting down the burden that is, quite literally, killing him. It's actually very good news.

Someone in the group said, "When you admit powerlessness, you get choice."

When William admits that he will die unless he gets help, he will be in a place where he gets to choose his help, where the bad news stops being a death sentence and becomes something much more like the truth that will set him free.

Right now the cynic has heard from the doctor, and the cynic has called the news a "death sentence." The cynic has summed up the situation with "So that's the way it is, then." He may as well have added "Amen."

William is acting out a script dictated to him by years and years of addictive thinking. And while I pray for him, I think it will take a miracle for God to break through William's defenses and coax him to choose the death of the cynic over the death of the man.

The good news is that, so far, William keeps coming back.

I was sitting two chairs away from William as he shared his story, and it shook me deeply. It made me realize that while there is no question the program has brought my insides back to life — I'd never realized they were dead until I started to see how different I'm being made — I'm still not doing many of the things I know I should be doing to improve my physical health.

I don't want to be the happy man, dead. The phrase keeps rattling around inside of me: *happy man, dead*.

I'm not going to the gym. That's the first one. And I enjoy the gym. I'm not intimidated being there. I like the simple workouts — which is a great benefit to being overweight, by the way; it takes a lot less exertion to achieve the same heart rate and effect. When I swim, I love that right now I am neutrally buoyant. I have enough fat on my body that I float. I could totally thrash my friend Dan the athlete in a contest of treading water because I don't have to move at all.

I don't go to the gym because some irrational part of me simply doesn't want to.

Same deal with a "food plan." That's another thing I should be doing but do not. Days that involve a whole pizza or some other huge meal are actually quite rare. I just don't pay attention and I eat too much, too often. I don't think a more structured system of eating would be that hard, and I know that I would feel better physically and emotionally if I ate carefully.

But there is some irrational part of me that just doesn't want to.

I think it's the cynic. I think I've tried enough other things in the past, and failed at them, and have so beaten myself up about them that I don't want to hear it anymore. The cynic doesn't believe I can change. Nor does that part of me want to get burned by the next failure. So the cynic tells me to sit still and risk nothing, to be smarter than the snares that have tripped me before and surely await me now. William made me see that I'm on the same path as he is, slave to the same brokenness of thought.

We all know this brokenness applies to far more than just my eating and my working out. This is a problem with the world in general, and with the Church in particular.

THE RIGHT PERSPECTIVE

A core, and huge, difference exists between the anthropology of Western philosophy and the affective — as in "affections" or "affectionate" — anthropology that's found in the Bible. The odds are good that you have spent your entire life bathed in Western philosophy rather than biblical anthropology, just as I have.

When it comes to who we are as people and how we navigate our lives, both schools of thought break us into three parts: the heart, the mind, and the will.

In the affective anthropology of the Bible, each part has a single capacity. The heart, our moral center, is the single source of our motives. It takes in stimuli and reaches value conclusions (evaluations) about what surrounds or indwells us. The heart is the source of our motivation, and its output passes to the instrumental faculties of the mind and the will. The mind uses the values from the heart to make judgments, process options, and pass the conclusions to the will, which applies the mind's best judgment into action.

In Western philosophy, all three faculties provide motivation in generating choices, and create a sort of internal dialogue within us. The trick becomes how to choose between the varied internal voices of heart, mind, and will. According to Western philosophy, the heart is distorted and our affections are ignoble. The will is damaged by sin. The mind is reliable if it is disciplined. Western philosophy reached these conclusions because the mind and will are seen as evident in God, while the heart and affections are not seen as present in a God who is "unmoved" or impassible. In classical theism, the will is "enabled" by grace as the mind and will overcome the faulty heart to make "good" decisions.

Another way of thinking of this is that in Western philosophy, and in our current principle-driven Christianity, we are to somehow pry ourselves away from ourselves so that we can get an objective look at ourselves. The assumption is that if we can just get a little distance, we'll be able to see what we need to work on, and then we can reengage ourselves and fix things up.

William the obese chemist has tried that. I've tried that. Heck, we've all tried that.

The problem is deeper than knowledge, and it's deeper than will. It's deeper than what we can fix on our own.

This is good news.

It's good news if we're able to pull away from the truly cynical self-objectification that's so common in our talk about things like "discipleship."

The Bible presumes our grasp on affective anthropology. While it makes no attempt to consistently link motives to conduct in one-to-one relationships, the Bible says that God always judges our conduct on the basis of our underlying motives (as do our modern courts, by the way). What that means is threefold. First, it means that the motives and intentions of our hearts are the pivotal concern of ethics. Second, it means that the way we read the Bible and the way we relate to one another should be much more sensitive to the biblical language of motivation. And finally, it means that we're going at this whole thing backwards, and that we can never get to the real source of our deadness by the hard scouring of mere principles; they simply can't reach far enough.

All covenants are God initiated and God fulfilled. Covenants create the context for the work of the Holy Spirit in our hearts, where our motives are reshaped. The mind of Christ will be ours as the heart of Christ beats within us — not the other way around. The living out of our faith will come because something changes within us.

What does this kind of change look like?

Reshaped

Start with the Greatest Commandment, to love the Lord God with all you've got and to love others as yourself. Move from there back to the Ten Commandments. Then go anywhere you see what feels like a "should" and say it back to yourself more like this offer or promise from God:

"When I'm the one who has reshaped your heart, you will ..."

"When I'm the one who has reshaped your heart, you will have no other gods before me, because you will love me with all you've got, and you will not be double minded or tossed about on the rough seas."

"When I'm the one who has reshaped your heart, you will love others as yourself because I do and I will cause you to."

"When I'm the one who has reshaped your heart, you will no longer feel inadequate and envious."

"When I'm the one who has reshaped your heart, you will honor your mother and father because I will make it possible."

Our part of the covenant is to answer the question God is asking us: "Do you want life like I'm talking about?"

If we say yes, the work begins. By the way, the effort required to let God do work in your heart is maybe, if even, 1 percent of what it takes to do it New Year's Resolution style.

If we say no, the need persists and the cynic continues to encounter moments where truth feels like a death sentence, and where addictions continue to grow until the cynic breaks, calls out, or, as happens far too often, dies.

In either case, the best we can do is to keep coming back.

Discussion Questions

1. Do you believe that you are powerless over your sin?

2. Over what things do you have power?

3. What is the difference between power and choice?

4. What benefit comes to the person who believes God judges conduct on the basis of motives? What pitfalls do you see to this approach? For whom is this basis of judgment *bad* news?

5. What "should" statement would you most like to experience as good news by adding "when I'm the one who has reshaped your heart ..." to the front of it?

6. Where would you like to see intimacy with God reshape your behaviors?

So if the Son sets you free,
you will be free indeed.
JOHN 8:36

PART III

SLAVES

CHAPTER 6

The Poseur:
In It to Win It

My dad was twenty-three when I was born. He'd been married two years, one month, and twelve days. He was a pharmacist at the hospital where I was born, Kenosha Memorial, about an hour north of Chicago, just across into Wisconsin.

He had no idea what he was doing.

None of us do, really; but as a kid I didn't know that.

Early Years

My first brother was born seventeen months after I was. Six weeks after that, my dad left the hospital and took a job in Duluth, Minnesota, selling pharmaceuticals for the company that ended up employing him for the rest of his career. He took the Duluth territory because it was the option that was closest to his father, who was sick with leukemia in Bismarck, North Dakota. His mother thought he was nuts, and so did my mother's parents. He had a perfectly respectable, stable job that paid well. The sales job meant a significant pay cut and a lot of time away from home because the territory was enormous and there were no interstates to use back then, just two-lane options, crowded with fishermen and family campers. His father thought he may be making a mistake too, but he understood that my dad needed to do what he needed to do, and he left it at that.

Within a couple of years we were back in Wisconsin, in a suburb of Milwaukee called Waukesha. The leukemia had driven my grandfather to North Carolina for treatment, so my dad transferred to the smaller territory. My grandfather passed away about a year later. Not long after that, when I was four years old, my youngest brother was born. I remember watching from the front window of our little ranch house as my parents returned from the hospital. I remember my mom getting out of the big burgundy LTD, cradling my brother in her arms in lieu of a child seat. My dad helped guide her by the elbow.

Dad had just turned twenty-eight, had a wife and three boys, and had no father to ask the hard questions. He was feeling his way through as he went. I think about everything he was facing at twenty-eight and compare that to what I felt like, and thought I knew, at twenty-eight, and it's hard not to conclude my dad had no business being in that position. So much was at stake. Being that young with that much to handle, he was bound to make the sorts of mistakes that leave marks on people's souls.

He worked hard at his job and did it well. My mother was proud of him. She was good at making him feel rewarded for his successes. I think that's a remarkable form of love, the kind that celebrates.

Running Away

We moved to Indianapolis on my eighth birthday. Dad bought a bigger house. He left when it was still dark outside, and he returned home after it was dark again.

The move was difficult for me. I had a hard time making friends. One day I got into a fight on the playground with two boys. The teacher who broke us up assumed that I'd started it because I was winning. I tore away from her and ran. I followed the train tracks that bordered the playground. As I crossed the White River, roiling and tumbling beneath the trestle, I remembered the news reports about dead bodies being found in it. When I got to the far side of the river, the vice principal pulled up beside me in his Camaro and told me I should hop in or I'd miss the school bus.

My mom picked me up from school. She drove home angry, which meant fast and in silence. She told me to sit on the couch and not move, that my dad would be home in a couple of hours and he'd be taking care of me.

He arrived home and heard about the day while he poured himself a drink. Then he came and sat down on the fireplace near the end of the couch. He told me that if I ever pulled a stunt like running away again, I'd get the spanking of my life. Then he sent me to my room until dinner.

At school I became known as the kid who had run away. Even the first graders would ask if I was the one. I was miserable.

Nobody had asked what was wrong. Or maybe I didn't have the words to answer when I was asked. All I know is that I *felt* as though nobody asked. Whatever solution I was expecting didn't come.

I figured it had something to do with me. Something wrong. Something bad.

Moving On

Two years later we moved to Seattle when my dad accepted a job as sales manager. That was spring break of fifth grade. The house was nicer, but the job was even more consuming. One year he spent something like two hundred nights in hotel rooms. He was big into self-improvement during this time, a true product of the eighties. Things went well for him. Except for the occasional botched hiking trip, anyway.

When he was home, dinner hour was a big deal. I remember paying close attention to everything about my dad, eager to be like him. One of the big things was being able to eat as much as he did. It meant I was a grown-up, like him. The trade-off was that my sports jerseys grew tight on me. One year I weighed too much to play Pee-Wee football; I was too heavy for the safety of the other kids. I remember crying on the front steps after I failed to lose the required weight. It had been weeks of effort, such as I could muster, and my mom came out to console me. My dad's response was that it was a good disappointment for me, maybe it would teach me about the value of hard work and self-discipline. What I was learning was that failure was grounds for punishment and paternal abandonment.

Teachers began to pay attention to me because of my writing. I don't know why it didn't seem to be worth anything at home, but it wasn't. I think my parents had their own distractions. Maybe they didn't have any basis for evaluating our life other than grades and our continued survival.

My memory is a little foggy, but I do remember that it was during junior high that something began to shift. In third grade, the experience of my runaway day had taught me to think of myself as inadequate. By junior high, after the hiking trip and the failure to lose weight to play football, I began to believe that I could never earn adequacy by anybody's rules.

We moved back to Indianapolis, to Zionsville, during Thanksgiving break of my freshman year of high school. Seattle's schools were about six months behind Zionsville's, so I was placed in remedial math, but was left in honors English. My dad talked about it being an opportunity for a fresh start for all of us. I wanted to earn his praise, and I took that opportunity seriously. He'd wrestled in high school, so I joined the team. I got pinned almost every time I stepped onto the mat. One time it took only eight seconds, and that included the referee counting to three. I looked up to the stands where my parents were sitting, and my dad was laughing. I don't remember him ever attending another match.

I quit at the beginning of my junior year when I was beat out of a varsity spot by a freshman who wasn't all that good. I got the quitter talk from dad when I got home.

By senior year, my papers were being read to the class as examples. Most every day I would write a story in study hall that would be passed to maybe a couple dozen kids, just for fun, before the notebook would be returned to me the next day. My dad said he thought I should be studying in study hall.

I felt like I was weird, and that I could never do enough to be okay. Even though I had significant successes, my dad spent his waking hours in a culture that preached such wisdom as, "If you're happy with the results you have, then you'll never get the results you want" or something like that. I never got a simple "good job." I got constructive criticism and suggestions for improvement. No victory felt like it counted.

GROWING UP

In college I partied in large part because I thought that's what I was supposed to do. Maybe because we'd never talked about what was expected of me, I thought "boys will be boys" was the approving response to the stupid sorts of behavior I was into. My dad seemed to enjoy the stories I told, even if his response often included things like, "There are some things a father doesn't need to know about."

After college, I landed a great job at an advertising agency. I was good at it. It was respectable and safe and it paid well. But it was the wrong place for me. I quit. My mother thought I was nuts. My father said that sometimes a man has to do what he has to do. I moved to Denver. I did ministry work and earned very little money. I was a source of worry and confusion for my parents.

I felt inadequate and clumsy. I felt like a dumbass. I felt like my dad didn't respect what I was doing, and no matter how well I argued the merits of my beliefs, he wasn't going to budge. Even where I was succeeding according to other people, it didn't translate as success to my dad, and because somewhere in my distant past I had come to see him as the only legitimate judge of what mattered and what didn't, even my successes felt like shame to me.

I moved back to Zionsville in the spring of my twenty-seventh year. I met a girl. I fell in love. My dad thought I needed to focus on finding and building a career, and that I needed to stop being so flaky. The girl took a job in Cleveland selling pharmaceuticals for the same company my dad had worked for. Three months later I announced that I was going to follow her. My dad thought that was a big mistake, and that I would get hurt if I moved for a girl. I moved anyway. I earned a certification as a network engineer so I could sell Cisco routers and switches. It was a smart job, and that was a decent sign for my dad.

My dad had been concerned about my move because I wasn't doing well. Just before I moved to Cleveland, I'd been diagnosed with anxiety after I spent a week sleeping on the couch in my apartment, afraid I was about to die. He paid for me to see a psychiatrist. I was put on Prozac. By the time I married the girl a year later, I'd gained eighty pounds.

I was a couple months past my twenty-ninth birthday the day of my wedding. Two months after that, the tech bubble burst and I was laid off. I spent six months looking for another job, but my skills were too new, and frankly I wasn't very good at the stuff. I couldn't find anything. I finally admitted that I was wired to write, and that I was going to go for it. All I meant at the time was that I would return to the advertising writing I'd once done, but that I'd do it for a Christian place and I'd do it with rules that respected God's place in my endeavors. My wife was livid because all I could find was work that paid peanuts. My dad was not too impressed either.

I was thirty-one when my wife transferred to a different pharmaceutical company to take a position back in Indianapolis. I was working on retainer with an out-of-town agency, so it didn't matter where I lived. We chose a place in Indianapolis, rather than Zionsville, where my parents, in-laws, and brothers' families and their in-laws all lived. We wanted something different in terms of lifestyle. Our choice was different from the choices our family had made, and for me, different could only feel wrong, weird, and cause for shame.

My wife and I had a hard time finding a church, which only added to the perception of my being weird, like I wasn't doing something right.

The Big Shift

I was angry.

I went to a counselor who told me I was angry. He said I was angry at my dad. About how I hadn't felt validated. How I hadn't felt seen for who I am. How I felt my dad had made me feel bad for who I am. How I felt he'd chosen his own desires and comforts over mine. How I had been the recipient of injustices. How when I was in pain he'd taught me to reject my own voice. The list went on and on. I blamed my dad for a lot of things.

Until one day. . .

My dad and I met in Zionsville for lunch. At the new sports bar that doesn't allow smoking and smells like the paint store next door in the strip mall. I felt tense. I was working on keeping my distance so that my time with him wouldn't set me off. I was practicing all of the boundary thoughts I'd picked up from my counselor and from discussions with my wife. My dad was the problem — caustic and ruinous. I was angry, but I was trying to be the bigger man.

I'd been working on my first book, and had self-published it, but nothing was "real" yet. I was terrified he'd poke and make me feel mocked about that.

Instead he started talking about his life. He was thinking about his impending sixtieth birthday. He seemed to be taking stock of his life. I was guarded but encouraged him. The conversation went as smoothly as it does between us. And then I could tell he was turning a corner to talk about a specific thing.

He asked about the recovery program I'd gotten into. I told him some things, guardedly, making sure not to give him anything to fix, and being careful not to try to recruit him to think my way.

And then he said it.

"It's weird, but for maybe the past six months I keep having this recurring prayer whenever I pray for you. Which is every day, by the way. I keep finding myself praying, 'God, I'm turning sixty this year, which means I have maybe twenty years left. I'd trade them all, and have you take me now, if you could help Pete lose two hundred pounds.'"

I think I just blinked a few times.

Then the moment passed with fairly matter-of-fact conversation. I think I said something like my bet being that God would let my dad live, and that he'd honor the other part of that prayer so that we would both see God's beauty and power.

But as I left that lunch, all I could think was "What in the world was *that*?"

It was a twisted boundary moment, for sure. What was I supposed to do with what he was saying? I mean, who says that sort of thing? It was selfish and just creepy.

And then the dam broke.

If the big, life-shaping crisis and parental failure happened when I was eight, then I'd spent twenty-seven years grooming my complaint about it. I'd been stewing in my anger. I'd pointed an accusing finger. I'd cursed my dad. I had felt hurt. I'd spent the majority of my life — *twenty-seven years* — being angry with him, feeling a righteous and tragic indignation about his failings.

But somewhere along the way, my dad had come to grieve for my living death — the death I was slowly, or not so slowly, pursuing with my addiction. For him it had gotten so bad that he was praying to trade away his retirement and his time with his wife and adult children and grandchildren because it hurt so much to watch me be this way.

I have taken full revenge, and then some. I have induced every bit of pain that I could ever want my father to feel in payment for the pain I've felt at his failures. And I never knew I was doing it. I was never aware of any satisfaction in it. I stole from my father. I hurt him. I caused him to grieve and ache for me, knowing I was in pain and knowing he was part of the cause. Suddenly I realized we were more than even.

All those years I'd taken solace in the posture of anger over my unjust wounding. All those years as victim had held me captive. I'd been a slave. A poseur with a sob story. I had been stealing from a man who finally reached the point, maybe without even knowing it, where he was crying out for mercy from me.

In my posing, I'd made him a slave too. And he was begging to be set free from my merciless tyranny.

That day God showed me that we'd done enough damage to each other. That day I added my father to the ever-growing list of people toward whom I make a point of living amends. I stole more from my father than he owed. As soon as I was able to give up my anger, I began to crave a salve for our wounds.

These days we're working on a new story of us.

Discussion Questions

1. Who taught you how to experience shame?

2. How has shame worked to protect you or serve you in your life?

3. What has shame cost you in your life?

4. How have you stolen revenge for the failures of other people?

5. How have you perpetuated the failures that hurt you?

CHAPTER 7

THE SQUEEZED DRY:
THE EDGES OF LOYALTY

People count on each other, whether that's parents and children, husbands and wives, or churches and congregations. And all the while, the pressures of justice and obedience to God bear both collective weight and individual weight upon us all. Take those pressures of dependence, relationship, and justice, and add brokenness and neurotic thinking into the mix, and good luck figuring out just how to be a loyal and loving partner.

It's been one thing for my father to struggle watching me, and it's been one thing for me to come to see that the issues between us are old and based on stale complaints. It is something entirely different with my wife. She is trying to figure out how much she can count on, and how to build with me. Her pain is the hardest pain in my world.

I'm changing inside. I am far more emotionally available than I've been. We enjoy one another like never before. But there is this undercurrent of sadness and a back-and-forth resentment between us. My addict thinking wants Christine to approve of everything I do, to pronounce every flaw and failure good. Christine is afraid of being a young widow, especially if we end up having kids. And right now, she's not willing to have kids with me because she doesn't want to risk parenting with a husband who can't run and jump with the kids, or who could soon be gone altogether. Dead.

She resents, and is sad about, that hard truth. I'm sad about not having kids. I'm sad about how she's missing out on one of her life dreams by being with me. I resent not getting to have things my way because she's drawn this line where she wants to have a husband who will survive long enough to be a good father.

My wife wants to honor me, wants to protect me, wants to respect me, and most of all wants to enjoy life with me. And I am failing her.

Christine's only way out of our resentment spiral — the only one she was willing to choose, the only one that didn't include getting rid of me completely — was to hand me over to God and to work on her own junk.

This is a good thing — maybe ultimately a required and holy thing — this giving of one's spouse to one's Lord, but she's told me it feels a lot like disloyalty and giving up, and I've told her it takes a lot of practice and patience before it quits feeling to me like the person giving the spouse to God is wishing bad things for the spouse. Me.

Being the one being given to God has a remarkable way of pressing every shame button in my world.

Over the past two years, Christine and I have given each other to God. We've concluded that the only way our marriage covenant will be fulfilled is if God makes it happen. After years of saying that all covenants are God initiated and God fulfilled, I finally saw just how true that is when I took my hands off the steering wheel in my own marriage. I don't ever want the steering wheel back. The marriage has become a partnership, a voluntary one. I love my wife like I can't even begin to describe, and her pain about me — caused by me — is still the hardest pain in my world.

Her pain is real. It is a statement of affirmation, something to work with. When I give up on everything else, the look of pain in Christine's eyes wakes me up and drives me to God like nothing else can.

It's not okay, just so we're clear. But it is what it is. I am what I am today, without defenses of "at least I'm not" or "who am I to complain?" I am an addict who desperately loves his wife, but has a proven track record of being unable to fix himself in an area that costs us both significantly. It is irrational. It is contradictory. It's also how most of life behind our masks of morality and "should-ing" on each other actually plays out.

The truth in my life, the truth of my addiction, haunts me, and the haunting only gets worse when I consider Bible stories like the one of Abigail and Nabal in 1 Samuel 25. The short version is this: David had protected Nabal's sheep and shepherds well when they'd been on David's turf, so David sends messengers to Nabal asking for a return of the favor. Nabal responds by asking, "Who is David?" and acts as though David is some young punk who doesn't deserve Nabal's respect.

Not cool.

David tells his men to strap on their swords, and they head out to put the smackdown on Mr. Big Britches Nabal and all of the men in his household. Justice is coming for the arrogant man.

Justice is always coming.

But Nabal's wife, Abigail, is intelligent and beautiful, and she knows that her husband is a bit of a dip. She hears about how Nabal treated David's men, and she understands the fate that's coming for Nabal in his arrogance. Abigail leaves home without telling Nabal where she's going, and she intercepts David on the way to wipe out her husband. She offers David the respect and the hospitality that he should have received from her husband, and she spares the house of Nabal the wrath that was heading its way.

Abigail doesn't tell Nabal about her meeting with David until the next day because, when she gets home, she finds Nabal drunk and feasting like a king. Like an arrogant king, with no business behaving like a king, completely ripe for some corrective justice. When Nabal hears what his wife did, he basically strokes out. Ten days later, he's dead.

Nabal dies, but none of his dependents suffer for his wicked ways.

Sort of like a fat man being denied kids by a wife who is determined to have better?

And then comes the real killer twist for a Nabal like me: Abigail marries David.

If I die, will Christine end up having kids with someone else?

If I die, will Christine's insistence upon health and boundaries be rewarded?

Can I escape the role, and the demise, of Nabal?

I pray that I might be spared such a fate.

But here are the real questions:

Was Abigail disloyal to Nabal?

Is Christine being disloyal to me?

What about when we zoom out to look at relationships between churches and congregations instead of relationships between husbands and wives? I can think of about a dozen past or present deacons at my church who have been completely squeezed dry by the Nabal-ish behaviors of my congregation. And maybe there are plenty of congregations these days, as new doctrines about who can and cannot be ordained are being charted in less than charitable or respectful tones, who feel squeezed dry by the Nabal-esque arrogance of their denominations.

Where we're Nabal, how do we muster the humility and the perspective to truly hear from our Abigails? What futures do we face if we neglect her wisdom?

Where we're Abigail, what is at stake if we choose loyalty to Nabal over loyalty to what is right? How much more will be lost when we add weak following to weak leadership?

We live in a broken world. There are broken leaders and there are broken followers, and love keeps them bound one to another even in their brokenness. There are too few answers, and even though David represents justice here, and is the good guy with whom Abigail eventually rides off into the sunset, David expresses relief that Abigail spared him the torment of taking vengeance with his own hand. Nabal's brokenness was going to cost David something, and part of that cost would have been rooted in David's own brokenness. David would have delivered justice to Nabal, but ultimately Nabal's arrogance would have called out David's.

We are all a mix of Nabal, Abigail, David, and the people who had no voice in the story — who were merely tied to the dramatic events by association to Nabal, to Abigail, or to David, but had their lives on the line nevertheless.

For those of us who, like my wife who loves me but suffers for what my addictions cost her, feel the enslavement and voicelessness of being tied to brokenness, sometimes healing feels a lot like disloyalty because sometimes the choice of obedience to God means that the Nabals in our lives don't get exactly what they demand.

We have no choice but to risk and to love, to live with and to sacrifice for the broken people in this world.

But there is nothing to be gained in being slaughtered by the enemies of a fool.

The Lord your God will certainly make a lasting dynasty for my lord, because you fight the Lord's battles, and no wrongdoing will be found in you as long as you live.... When the Lord has fulfilled for my lord every good thing he promised concerning him and has appointed him ruler over Israel, my lord will not have on his conscience the staggering burden of needless bloodshed or of having avenged himself.

1 Samuel 25:28, 30 – 31

DISCUSSION QUESTIONS

1. Where do you give until you are "squeezed dry"?

2. What benefit do you gain for giving too much?

3. Who are the Nabals in your life? The Abigails? The Davids? Where are you a nameless person caught in the crossfire? Where do you create crossfire that impacts the people who are vulnerable to your choices?

4. What would a choice for intimacy with God look like in that situation?

CHAPTER 8

The Elder Brother:
The Slavery of Silence

A friend called the other day. He's working on a series of essays about faith and art and wanted to know my thoughts on some of what he's exploring. It's a topic I've thought about, writing as I am for a Christian publisher, being shelved in the Christian book section, yearning to be relevant and compelling, especially to Christians.

I think much of life as a believer comes down to this: does Christianity modify us, or do we modify Christianity? I don't mean does grace transform us. I mean, am I a Christian writer, or a writer dealing with Christianity? Is it better to think in terms of Christian artists, or is it better to think of artistic Christians?

I can't make sense of a Christian murderer — meaning someone who murders as evidence of his faith. But one of the things I love about the God I'm getting to know is that he has absolutely no problem making room for a murderer Christian — as in a Christian who has murdered. Sin does not disqualify us from our adoption into the family of our heavenly Father. The deepest, most indelible part of a person's identity comes from the space that's occupied by God. He claims the profound center and leaves no room for any god beside him. And it's the fact that he knows where his authority lives that makes him so gracious about the rest of who we are.

Christianity is not some glaze we apply over the top of other things. Christianity is this amazing core that we find happily inside anything touched by anyone who will welcome the Spirit inside.

"Christian" isn't what modifies us. We modify "Christian."

INSIDER'S PREROGATIVE

My last name comes with a family history. It stands for things in my world. There are stories that tell me who I am, that shape the way I see life, and that I hold in common with both my immediate family and my extended family. But my last name does not define me, it merely labels me and grounds me. A Gall is whatever I am because I am called Gall. The meaning of the name, of the word, comes from how I live my life while bearing that name.

The hard part comes when my choices don't feel good to other people with the same name. For example, I'm not writing this book in a vacuum. Other people, including my father, are reading each draft, and the versions they're reading are not as delicate or considerate as the version that will end up on bookshelves. The stories I'm including haven't been easy for either my father or me to engage. And while my dad and I are learning a new way of interacting, it's been hard for my mom to see the price we're paying for our recent interactions. It's good stuff, exciting — liberating, even — but it hurts along the way. I am clearly breaking the rules that have existed, to whatever extent they've been articulated in the past, about how we do things in the Gall family.

People are often led to say things in ways that are contrary to the old rules, in families and in extended families like the body of Christ. It's hard to be the one speaking. Sometimes it's hard to be the one listening. And it's hard to be the people, like my mother or my wife in the instance of what's happening between my dad and me, who see how much both sides are paying in their attempts at having love and hopeful truth find a way to coexist.

But what else can we do? If we don't make room for the whole family to speak, the family name becomes not only meaningless, but a very small, very manipulated prison.

My dad, even with all of the misinterpretations about myself or about the world, and how much of that I lay at his feet, is letting me speak. He is interacting with me, even though it is hugely expensive to him. It hurts, but we still meet for long lunches. We still trade very careful emails. We still work to understand. And we reach the end of our understanding; he's teaching me how to simply let love be stronger than all temptations to the contrary.

Firstborn Fears

I have played the role of prodigal son before, in my twenties. I have been delivered home by brothers who borrowed my father's SUV for the task. But now I have been around for years, and in many ways I have become the elder son.

These days, the story I wish I could hear from Jesus is what happened when the elder son, the one who stayed home when the prodigal had his adventure and who experienced confusion at his father's excitement when the prodigal brother returned, finally gained his voice and spoke up.

The negative things I learned from my dad — the stuff that led to my self-doubts and neurotic thinking about the world — were from a different time in his life, from a father who had not yet had a very real "change of heart" by God's working. The guy I know today is radically different. I not only love him, he's one of my favorite people, someone from whom I have so much to learn and to whom I owe so much. I enjoy being with him, just for the sake of being with him.

Perhaps like the elder brother in Jesus' parable, I have no desire to be removed from my father. I prize knowing him far above whatever inheritance the prodigal son may have seen. I don't want to go anywhere. And yet, I remember moments of pain; and I know that so long as I stay silent, I will stay trapped in a place that must be similar to the place where the elder son found himself.

What do you do if you really like the father, but it hurt you and confused you when he threw the feast for the prodigal brother? It's cool that the younger brother is home and everything, but the prodigal wasted his inheritance, and now he'll get another chunk. Or he'll make you look like a jerk if you don't help him out when Dad's gone. Family dynamics are messy. How do you tell Dad how you feel? Is it right to say anything about it and make him feel bad? Is it right to say nothing and to feel the shameful frustration fester? What do you do?

What do you say if your own healing comes by admitting failures someone else doesn't want you to acknowledge? How much will it cost you if you say nothing?

What do you say about a church culture that has been worth loving but has been unable to make room for its own failures? What do you say about a church culture that is doing good things in the world but has proven itself willing to "break a few eggs to make an omelet" and you've been one of the eggs?

What do you say to a God who has given his only Son, who died nailed to a cursed tree for your sins, whose Spirit lives within you, and who longs to spend eternity with you — but who still won't speak to you in an audible voice, still won't stop the AIDS in Africa, still lets the bad guys roam free, and still won't make the dark nights less scary?

The prodigal son was a fool, but he was restored and, in the process, he learned something that's terrifying for elder brother personalities to test. What is that thing, that truth? What does the prodigal son know that his elder brother has yet to learn?

The love of your Father is far more durable than you've come to believe. Your voice is his joy, and your heart is his treasure, and he will pay any price to know you.

Tell him. Tell him where it hurts. Tell him what you experienced, and what you concluded. Ask him if that's what he intended for you to conclude about him. He can take it. And his willingness to take it is an expression of love that validates every hard, obedient choice you've ever made — because you have been serving a Father who is worth serving with hard, obedient choices.

The Father's response to the honest voice of the elder son is the best proof I know for the character of God. Therefore, the honest voice of the elder son is the best demonstration of the Father's glory the elder son can ever deliver. The elder son's honest voice is, in fact, the elder son's most outstanding demonstration of obedience to a Father who bids us come and who promises to love us no matter how turned around we may feel.

Tell him.

Discussion Questions

1. How does who you are modify *Christian*?

2. Where has God left you in pain or in some other way sent you a message that confused you?

3. Where have the people of God wounded you in God's name?

4. *The love of the Father is far more durable than you've come to believe.* Do you believe it? What questions or accusations do you have for him to test it? (Be warned: if you test God's love and it turns out to be durable enough for you, you will find yourself in intimate relationship with him. Do you want intimacy with God?)

CHAPTER 9

THE LEPER:
LOVE'S LOUD VOICE

I have a little diagram next to my keyboard to help me remember the themes I want to hit in these chapters. The section about tyrants was intended for people whose deep craving is to hear God say, "You are adequate exactly as you are." I think tyrants tend to be cruel because they fear the loss of control and the judgment against them. This section about slaves is intended for people who long to hear God say, "Your voice matters." Slaves tend to forget they're wired for better than fear and mere coping techniques.

UNCLEAN

I think Satan's favorite perversion is to distort how we use our voices, so that we use our voices to cry out a warning to people who may fear contamination by our sins, especially our pasts. In the Bible, lepers were required to warn people, from a distance, that they were "unclean."

Anyone with such a defiling disease must wear torn clothes, let their hair be unkempt, cover the lower part of their face and cry out, "Unclean! Unclean!" As long as they have the disease they remain unclean. They must live alone; they must live outside the camp.

LEVITICUS 13:45 – 46

"Tah-may!" they would call out. "Unclean!" Stay away! We will pollute you. We will ruin your world.

I hang out with a variety of people who have a variety of addictions. For each of us there is a stage in the recovery process where the addiction has been admitted, but grace does not yet feel strong enough to trust. At this stage, addicts have a tendency to proclaim "unclean!" or some other warning that has to do with the fact that we have come to see that contingent beings living in a fallen world cannot make promises. It takes an honest sinner a while to learn that God lives his promises through those who will let him.

Addicts aren't the only ones who struggle to spot the saint instead of the sinner, are they? Life teaches us all to watch for weak places in one another. I think about uncleanness when I see a heavy person pick a chair, when I see a recovering drug addict fidget, when I see an alcoholic laugh just a little too loudly, when I shake a porn addict's hand, when a co-dependent person asks me how I'm doing, or when some church ladies ask for prayer requests. Maybe I have the thoughts because there is still a part of me that wants to grab the microphone and yell to the world, "*Tah-May*! Unclean!"

It feels a little noble too, this warning we call out, this self-sacrificing admission that we're not people to embrace. A sense of heroic martyrdom is associated with it, a sense that I'm taking one for the team when I tell you that I'm broken.

I suppose that's a sort of love, but mostly it's a way for me to have nothing to live up to. It's a way for me to let myself off the hook before the hook comes anywhere near me. It's a way for me to use my voice without ever risking a thing — especially risking telling the whole truth.

I get praise for writing "real" stuff. That's a big word these days, *real*. So is *authentic*. And *raw* even made it onto the cover of my first book. I'm really starting to hate those words. It seems like they're used to describe someone who'll talk about the broken places, the dirty places, the mess of life, like that's what's real. Like that's all that's real.

It's not. In fact, the "real" and "raw" messes of life — the broken places and the hurt places and the oh-so-shocking places — are barely even noteworthy aspects of life in a fallen and broken world. We all have pain. People hurt each other. Fear overwhelms our faith and our compassion until we choose the death of another over the discomfort we may otherwise have to stare down on our own. So what? Is that really news? It seems to me that the garbage is the backdrop, the given, the mundane and boring friction of life.

What's remarkable is that we still hope for something else. Something better.

Hope, I'm convinced, is the best sort of defiance in a world chock-full of misery.

Yelling "unclean" is really pretty boring. Yeah, yeah, we know. You're unclean. What else can you tell us about yourself?

WAR ZONE

A friend came to town to visit recently. He's been home from a tour in Iraq for a couple of years, and his experiences over there messed with him pretty bad. He led a convoy team of eight other men — three trucks with turret-mounted machine guns — to shuttle various commanders around the Tikrit area. There were gunfights, four or five per month, and sometimes that meant piling out of the trucks to fight. We didn't talk details beyond that, but he did tell me that war is hell, and that hell is the absence of God. He said there was no way God was present when he was seeing what he saw. And something about what he saw, and something about experiencing moments where he couldn't imagine God being present, have left him with new and frightening surges of anger to deal with.

We talked about the parallels between what he saw in the heat and the dust and the din of war, and what it would look like if someone could drive a Humvee through any moment of personal failure and sin. I told him that my whole experience of intentionally sinful moments — like when I need an hour alone to gnaw down a pepperoni pie — feel a lot like I'm shoving God out. I've heard friends talk about what it feels like to be drawn to the office in their home where they keep the computer and its Internet temptations. Others have described how much they wish they could smoke and melt into the sofa like they used to. And drinkers have told me about ingesting the bullets of booze and the grenades of destruction that come with the drunkenness. Those moments of being overrun by our sin are surreal. If someone were to drive through and see what's going on inside any of us during those moments, they would see a pretty good dose of senseless violence and pain without comfort.

"Do you think that's a fair comparison?" I asked my soldier friend.

"Yeah, I'd say that's fair. Except with war a whole bunch of people join in, and kids die."

That's a different sort of hell, we concluded. But there is hell in any sin, and it has something to do with ejecting God from a moment. It has something to do with believing the lie behind the cry we're taught: *"Tah-May!* Unclean!" And rolling with it for a time.

Again, though, that's not the remarkable thing.

My friend opened his computer and showed me photos and video clips of his time there. He showed me the eight men he'd commanded — all of whom survived, due to the prayers they prayed before their missions. Or at least that's what he believed while he was there, when he didn't take time to think about it too much. He knew other people who prayed and died anyway.

The eight men were fiercely frightening. The rifles were bigger than I was expecting. And as a group, standing around and upon a Humvee, they were intense. Deadly intense. They were from Missouri, and Indiana, and New Jersey. My friend told me some of their stories. He showed me a photo of the two guys who rode in his truck with him — definitely guys you'd want with you at the bar in case there was trouble. He showed me photos of camel spiders, nasty creatures that attack anything, even people. He told me how they'd catch smaller camel spiders and pit them against scorpions and how soldiers would bet on the outcome, like a sporting event. There were photos of the palaces. Of the Tigris River. Of smiles on men cleaning their guns. Of target practice out in the middle of nowhere. Of sunsets. Amazing, breathtaking sunsets.

He told me that it was strange to see sunsets there, or a sieve of stars in the night, when it was hell in moments during the day. It was like God was still there, above it all, able to rush back in as soon as there was room for him again.

My friend has been changed by his experiences. He has bad

dreams. He has moments of frightful anger. He has physical pain that stays with him, and has so far been refused treatment at a veterans hospital. He has emotional pain about the injustice he's experienced. Hints of that pain can be seen regarding choices of the military and the big picture of the war itself. He doesn't talk about the changes with a sense of gratitude, but he does have glimpses into what it means to be damaged goods when you're also loved by God. He understands how true strength begins to grow when you reach the end of yourself and see something beyond you doing something with you. And he likes it.

He does not yell "unclean!" to warn you about him, though there are broken places. Something, maybe something he can't quite put his finger on yet, tells him his voice is meant for better than that.

SICKNESS

Now on his way to Jerusalem, Jesus traveled along the border between Samaria and Galilee. As he was going into a village, ten men who had leprosy met him. They stood at a distance and called out in a loud voice, "Jesus, Master, have pity on us!" When he saw them, he said, "Go, show yourselves to the priests." And as they went, they were cleansed. One of them, when he saw he was healed, came back, praising God in a loud voice. He threw himself at Jesus' feet and thanked him — and he was a Samaritan. Jesus asked, "Were not all ten

cleansed? Where are the other nine? Was no one found
to return and give praise to God except this foreigner?"
Then he said to him, "Rise and go; your faith has made
you well."

LUKE 17:11 – 19

Jesus once healed ten leprous men and sent them to present
themselves to the priest to be proclaimed clean. Only one returned
to Jesus later. Why?

Imagine it: Let's say you're a middle-aged man with a wife and
a few kids and some sheep, and you develop leprosy. You lose everything. You lose feeling in parts of your body. You lose parts of your
body. You lose your family. You lose the right to travel near others.
You lose the right to travel quietly. You even lose the right to go to
the temple. You are left with only the company of other people who
suffer from the same sickness that has cost you everything. That's
how the story begins.

You do what you can to get by. You learn to deal with the special kind of emotional bitterness and destructiveness that is common
among people who have lost everything and whose bodies have gone
mostly numb. A cauldron of bile on the inside, and a deteriorating
heap of clay on the outside, those leper friends of yours.

This is light-years from what it feels like to be fat, or addicted to
whatever else people in today's world fall into. Right?

Life becomes a drudge. It's about coping. It's miserable.
Dreams shrivel and die and are not replaced. Lepers and addicts
know no springtime, only long, gray winters. You see your nose
going lumpy and sort of twisting a bit. Your hands thicken and freeze

and gnarl, and you feel it when a finger breaks, but then you don't feel it when it crumbles away. And you used to be so good-looking. You remember the way your wife used to look at you — used to *gaze* upon you — and the sorrow is too much to remember it any longer. You block that out.

And the whole deal about having to warn people that you are unclean and only being able to shout to them from a safe distance — it's more rotten than your skin. You know there is punishment if you don't follow that rule. Besides, you don't want anyone, anyone, to experience what you experience. So you call out, as loud as your failing chest will let you, *"Tah-May!* Unclean!" to warn them to keep their distance from you. You look horrible, even worse than you have to, because you're required to wear torn clothing and keep your hair messy so you'll be even easier to spot as diseased. You're required to cover the lower part of your face — your mouth, where your voice lives. It's not welcome anymore, except to cry "Unclean!" to strangers. Not that those restrictions are all that contrary to how you'd be anyway. You can't keep yourself and your clothing clean living as you do with the lepers, and you can't tell when your tunic is twisted or slipping from its place, and you walk funny now. Really, who cares?

So, yeah, life bumps along and is taking forever, and the pain spreads, but only just ahead of the numbness — so even the pain is a mixed bag because the wicked pain won't last forever, but the cessation of the pain will be even worse.

CALLING OUT

One day one of the people you hang out with and scrape by with tells you about this Jesus guy who's passing nearby. So you wander along with the group, smoking a cigarette because, again, who cares, and you see Jesus and his friends off in the distance. Always in the distance. You don't even remember what a normal face looks like because you haven't seen one in years. There's no way the guy's going to respond to the shouts of your group, but your friends start to yell, so what the heck, you yell too.

"Have mercy on us!" the cry goes out. And there is waving of robes and three-fingered hands and your friend Ilene — who looks more like a guy now, and is always being confused for one — is doing that weird thing she does where she hops on her one mostly good leg and leans crookedly against that stick she uses as a crutch. What an embarrassing group you've fallen into. But you're a good sport, so the words come out of your mouth too. "Master, have mercy on us!"

And Jesus turns and looks and he sees you, your broken silhouettes backlit on the hump of dirt you've been waiting on, and you hear this tiny, far-off voice that sounds a lot less masculine and smooth than you would have guessed from such a celebrity, and it says, "Go, show yourselves to the priests!"

Do what?

"Yeah," you say to your best friend, Tommy the Toe, "let me tell you about priests and how much fun they've been in my life. It was a priest who drove me out of town."

"But what if this is for real?" Tommy asks. "I'm goin'."

Ilene's going too. So's Matty Over There, and so is Say-What Sauly, the guy who lost his ears. Pretty soon everyone's going. So what else can you do? You head out with them.

It's a hot day, and it's going to be a long walk. Your sandals aren't great on the loose rock. Pretty soon your feet are killing you.

Your feet are killing you. What? You haven't heard from them in three years. It doesn't feel great, but it *feels*. You don't say anything, but you look around at the others to see if anything weird is happening with them. Anything weird in a group of lepers with names like Johnny Bowl-a-Chowda and Nicky the Nub? Go figure.

Ilene is crying and holding one hand in the other. She says she needs to sit down for a little bit. Nicky stays with her. He's crying too.

The rest of you keep going. Tommy the Toe asks if anyone else is feeling a little "odd."

Say-What Sauly nods. He looks around a little, like he's trying to find something. He stops. He hears a little bird singing in a rosemary bush, and is captivated. He whispers that he'll catch up with everyone else in a little bit.

You keep going. Your skin is on fire. Your feet are torture. You feel the tears from the agony. Another mixed bag. It's always a mixed bag, pain and comfort. But you say nothing. You don't want to jinx it. You're going to the priest, and you're going right now.

Johnny Bowl-a-Chowda starts hyperventilating. He starts trembling. Matty Over There asks what's wrong.

"I can't go home. I can't go home! There's nothing there for me anymore. And look at me! Where will I go? What did that man do to us? What were we thinking? Where will I go now?"

Tommy the Toe says, "If you don't want to go home, just go back to the camp."

"I can't do that either! If I'm healed, I can't be around the leper camp! What if I caught it again? What would that do to the person who passed it to me? Nobody there will want to be near me! What am I going to do now?" And Johnny drops to the ground in a heap.

"You guys go ahead," Matty says. "We'll meet you later."

By the time you get to the edge of town, it's just you and Tommy the Toe. The pain has swept over your body so many times that it doesn't even hurt anymore. You call to a young boy and ask him to find the priest. You wait in the shade of a small tree. You've been feeling your skin burning in the sun. Feeling it, but not testing it. You start thinking about your wife. Her eyes. Her long black hair. Home. You are actually thinking about home. Softness. Sweetness. Could it be? You feel Tommy the Toe nudge your elbow with his.

"Look," he whispers, and he pushes his chin out in front of him to gesture. At first you assume he sees a snake. You look. You don't notice right away, but then ... there are nine tiny new toe nubs pushing their way out from his feet.

The priest and his young assistant arrive, a cloud of incense and sweat and grilled meat smells engulfs you. He gives you and Tommy the Toe, with his new set of phalanges and a recent request for a new nickname, the once-over. You both have scars, but after a few minutes he shrugs and says, "You seem pretty healed to me."

The Lord said to Moses, "These are the regulations for any diseased person at the time of their ceremonial cleansing, when they are brought to the priest: The priest is to go outside the camp and examine them. If they have been healed of their defiling skin disease, the priest shall order that two live clean birds and some cedar wood, scarlet yarn and hyssop be brought for the person to be cleansed. Then the priest shall order that one of the birds be killed over fresh water in a clay pot. He is then to take the live bird and dip it, together with the cedar wood, the scarlet yarn and the hyssop, into the blood of the bird that was killed over the fresh water. Seven times he shall sprinkle the one to be cleansed of the defiling disease, and then pronounce them clean. After that, he is to release the live bird in the open fields.

"The person to be cleansed must wash their clothes, shave off all their hair and bathe with water; then they will be ceremonially clean. After this they may come into the camp, but they must stay outside their tent for seven days. On the seventh day they must shave off all their hair; they must shave their head, their beard, their eyebrows and the rest of their hair. They must wash their clothes and bathe themselves with water, and they will be clean.

"On the eighth day they must bring two male lambs and one ewe lamb a year old, each without defect, along with three-tenths of an ephah of the finest flour mixed with olive oil for a grain offering, and one log of oil. The priest who pronounces them clean shall present both the one to be cleansed and their offerings before the Lord at the entrance to the tent of meeting.

"Then the priest is to take one of the male lambs and offer it as a guilt offering, along with the log of oil; he shall wave them before the Lord as a wave offering. He is to slaughter the lamb in the sanctuary area where the sin offering and the burnt offering are slaughtered. Like the sin offering, the guilt offering belongs to the priest; it is most holy. The priest is to take some of the blood of the guilt offering and put it on the lobe of the right ear of the one to be cleansed, on the thumb of their right hand and on the big toe of their right foot. The priest shall then take some of the log of oil, pour it in the palm

of his own left hand, dip his right forefinger into the oil
in his palm, and with his finger sprinkle some of it before
the Lord seven times. The priest is to put some of the
oil remaining in his palm on the lobe of the right ear of
the one to be cleansed, on the thumb of their right hand
and on the big toe of their right foot, on top of the blood
of the guilt offering. The rest of the oil in his palm the
priest shall put on the head of the one to be cleansed
and make atonement for them before the Lord.

LEVITICUS 14:1 – 18

CLEAN

From here the rituals begin. You didn't even know there was a ritual
for ceremonial cleansing of healed lepers, but once you think about
it, it's not a big surprise. There are rituals for everything.

The priest sends the assistant back down the hill into town on
the craziest scavenger hunt you've ever heard. Hyssop, scarlet yarn,
cedar wood, two clay pots of fresh water, and two white doves for you
and two for Tommy. The boy is gone for an hour, during which time
the priest asks how you were healed.

"We yelled to Jesus of Nazareth, and he yelled back that we
should present ourselves to you," Tommy Ten Toes says.

"Ah. So it is a mystery then," the priest replies, and the subject
is explored no further.

When the priest's assistant returns, he places a pot of water on
the ground in front of you. The priest withdraws one of the white

doves from its cage, pulls out a small knife, and cuts the bird's throat. You and Tommy exchange quick glances. It is the first expense anyone has incurred on your behalf in you don't even remember how long.

The blood from the bird trickles into the water in dark swirls of shadow and ripple. You swallow. The priest reaches for the second bird.

He ties a splinter of cedar and twig of hyssop, with its dried blue flower, to the dove's leg with the red yarn. Then, holding the dove in both hands, he dips it into the bloody water, and pulls it out. The dove does not struggle. Water streams over its head and back into the bowl. And you remember the caress of your wife. The priest plunges the bird into the water seven times, and you hold your breath each time, your eyes locked with the dove's black, placid eyes. You remember laughter. Blankets. Your baby's cheek on yours. Hot baths. Smooth wood. Puppy fur. By the seventh emersion, the bird is pink where you can see feathers — its head, tail, and the tips of its wings.

"I pronounce you clean," the priest says. Then he tells you to hold out your hand, palm up. He gently places the dove on your palm. The dove, with its pink head, tail, and wingtips, left white only where the priest's hands kept it dry, stares straight into your eyes. It cocks its head. And then in a rush of wings and fluttering sounds, it takes flight.

You will have scars, you realize, as you watch the pink of the bird in the sky. The bird's mate, its other half, its second self, dead with only bloodstained feathers in your bird left as legacy. But you are free.

There are more ceremonies. The shaving of your hair and the washing of your clothing is first, with a sacrifice and blood and oil on your right earlobe, thumb, and big toe to come on the eighth day. During the eight days, you wait. You think about the meaning of the ceremony with the lobe and the thumb and the toe. Tommy laughs that he could have done that one all along. Why the right side? Why the ear, thumb, and toe? Something feels tied to the two birds, to the self that has always endured, and the passing of the part that is being laid aside, killed, remembered only in quiet and grimly sacred tones. You are reminded of the doorway markings during Passover, but you can't quite put that one together. The townspeople know in their minds that you're clean, but you're not all the way clean quite yet, and you know that to them you may never be clean enough. Scars will linger in your interactions with them as well.

Matty Over There, Nicky the Nub, Irene, and the others make their way in during the eight days. Say-What Sauly arrives on the fourth day. At first he doesn't recognize you. He stares, puzzling you out, trying to place you and figure out which of his friends you are. You grin, delighting in the moment, in being a renewed creature an even old friend can't recognize. But there is something familiar, and finally he says, "Numbass, is that *you?*"

But you've been healed. You know the only answer you can give to your friend.

"God doesn't call me Numbass."

Healing hurts. But it's better than learning not to feel anything. And I don't know what to make of the fact that in the Bible's version of this story, only one leper — a Samaritan, an outsider, a nonchurch person, a reject among rejects — comes back to Jesus to throw himself at Jesus' feet to thank him.

But what I do know is this: The Bible says he came back with "a loud voice."

Was it a habit he picked up from having to yell to be heard as a leper?

Was it a new joy in being able to yell good news instead of the old word?

Doesn't matter. All I care about is being a healed leper with a loud voice that praises the God who shed blood for my deliverance.

DISCUSSION QUESTIONS

1. In what ways are you unclean?

2. How do you keep people away from your shame? How do you call out "Unclean"?

3. In what ways do you have scars from your unclean experience?

4. In what ways have the people of God taught you that your voice was unwanted?

5. Where have you seen regeneration or healing in your world?

6. What does "your voice matters" look like in your world?

7. Where would you like to have a louder voice?

8. What do you have to say?

[Oh, Sweetheart], who told you that you were naked?

FOOLS

CHAPTER 10

THE PRODIGAL:
PERSONAL LOVE, INHERITED IDENTITY

Jesus continued: "There was a man who had two sons. The younger one said to his father, 'Father, give me my share of the estate.' So he divided his property between them.

"Not long after that, the younger son got together all he had, set off for a distant country and there squandered his wealth in wild living. After he had spent everything, there was a severe famine in that whole country, and he began to be in need. So he went and hired himself out to a citizen of that country, who sent him to his fields to feed pigs. He longed to fill his stomach with the pods that the pigs were eating, but no one gave him anything.

"When he came to his senses, he said, 'How many of my father's hired servants have food to spare, and here I am starving to death! I will set out and go back to my father and say to him: Father, I have sinned against heaven and against you. I am no longer worthy to be called your son; make me like one of your hired men.' So he got up and went to his father.

"But while he was still a long way off, his father saw him and was filled with compassion for him; he ran to his son, threw his arms around him and kissed him.

"The son said to him, 'Father, I have sinned against heaven and against you. I am no longer worthy to be called your son.'

"But the father said to his servants, 'Quick! Bring the best robe and put it on him. Put a ring on his finger and sandals on his feet. Bring the fattened calf and kill it. Let's have a feast and celebrate. For this son of mine was dead and is alive again; he was lost and is found.' So they began to celebrate.

"Meanwhile, the older son was in the field. When he came near the house, he heard music and dancing. So he called one of the servants and asked him what was going on. 'Your brother has come,' he replied, 'and your father has killed the fattened calf because he has him back safe and sound.'

"The older brother became angry and refused to go in. So his father went out and pleaded with him. But he answered his father, 'Look! All these years I've been slaving for you and never disobeyed your orders. Yet you never gave me even a young goat so I could celebrate with my friends. But when this son of yours who has squandered your property with prostitutes comes home, you kill the fattened calf for him!'

"'My son,' the father said, 'you are always with me, and everything I have is yours. But we had to celebrate and be glad, because this brother of yours was dead and is alive again; he was lost and is found.'"

LUKE 15:11 - 32

If someone could live on the family farm, do work they loved, be safe and provided for, and feel both fulfilled and completely in agreement with all of the family rules, you'd expect them to stick around, right?

So why do you suppose the younger brother would ask for his inheritance and leave?

Something about feeling stir crazy on the farm? A yen to see the world? Maybe the problem had something to do with not feeling challenged by the work he was doing, something about farm work being boring? Perhaps the younger brother didn't know what his inheritance would be, and he didn't know what to expect from the future? Maybe he didn't like his father's rules? Didn't like being pushed around? Didn't like feeling second fiddle to the elder brother?

My guess is that the younger brother didn't start out with any intention to leave at all. The story says he didn't leave right away. My guess is that he started out simply wanting to know that he was loved and that he mattered and that his father would give him freedom if that's what the son wanted. I think he just wanted to know that he could count on his father's promises. And when the father let the son have his inheritance ... well, then the possibilities began to swirl.

I think the younger son had a simple crisis of faith. He forgot something about who his father was, and the father's proof came too easily for the son to see its worth and meaning, so he took off.

I think this because the prodigal son didn't head toward anything. He merely left. It wasn't that he wanted more than life with the family; he just wanted to try life on his own. He had the power and the means to go, so he went. If the son had left to explore or to take his shot at something, that might be different. But he didn't. He just cashed in and blew it all on "wild living."

Unseen and Undervalued

I'm glad to have this story. The prodigal son is somebody I can relate to. I think a lot of people who have met the Father forget just how easily he shares his wealth, and at what little cost to us. I think a lot of us have a hard time dealing with a God who is that generous and that selfless. Some of us become elder sons, unwilling to tell the Father what's really going on inside of us for fear of losing our place with him. Others react to the shame of being blessed for what seems like no good reason, and in our sense of fraud or failure, we reject the Father before he can reject us.

This morning I was in a recovery workshop with someone who talked about how she works extra hard at things because she knows she'll never be the pretty one or the skinny one, so in an effort to at least be remembered, she offers to lead things. She takes on tasks, burns the midnight oil, smiles all the time, and laughs even when she's telling heart-wrenching stories (because everyone loves a friendly girl, and nobody likes a weepy fat one). She's afraid of being ignored. She's afraid that she's invisible to God and to the world. She's afraid that no matter how hard she works or how good she is, she will never earn the adoration of the crowd. And if the people never notice her and nobody remembers her, her life will be like a tree falling in the woods with no one to hear it. Her life will make no sound at all.

She's a classic example of the elder son.

I'm like that sometimes. Sometimes I feel as though I'm unseen and undervalued. Sometimes I work hard to be noticed, and sometimes I make rebellious noise for the sake of being heard. But for the most part, I find myself struggling with my responses to what has often felt like unmerited adoration. I have more frequently chosen the response of the prodigal.

Underachiever! Exactly.

I am the firstborn, and that's resulted in my being treated differently. Maybe not better — my parents love us all the same, of course — but it's a subtle thing for a kid to tell the difference between "different" and "favored."

My elementary school teachers showed me special attention for my writing. I didn't like it. It made me feel singled out, and "singled out" feels a lot like "picked on" when you're eight or ten.

I was a good Little League pitcher, and coaches paid special attention to me.

When I was a junior in high school, I was in the same French class as my freshman brother. The guidance counselor showed up in our classroom looking for me one day. The kids all made "oohs" and "aahs" like I was in trouble. The counselor's protective response was to announce, "Pete is a national merit scholar, which means that he's smarter than all of you." I noticed my brother's smile twist a little. The counselor said all sorts of clumsy flattering junk to me on the way to his office. Then he pulled out my transcripts and saw my 2.8 GPA and launched into this rant about "You've got to be about the biggest underachiever I've ever met!"

"Exactly" was my point. So shut up.

I played football, and even though I was never very good at it, the team was. The whole town would come out for games. One year Halloween fell on a Friday, and the trick-or-treating was moved to Saturday so it wouldn't conflict with the game. One time I was stopped for speeding, but I had my jersey on, so I was let go and wished good luck. There were "hall walks" where all of the other students would be let out of class early so they could line the halls and pat the football team on our backs as we made a lap through the school. I remember passing my brother one time. He was in band. The school didn't do hall walks for band.

Youth group.

Girlfriends.

Drinking buddies in college.

Professors.

An incredible job coming out of college.

Good fortune during five years in Denver.

Family that took me back in.

A wife I can barely reference in this light without tears of humbled gratitude, and a voice in my head that tells me she's way too good for me.

I get to write books for a living, for crying out loud. I drive home after a long day of doing what I love doing more than anything else in the world, and totally don't get why I've been blessed this way.

Despite my inability to receive it, and despite the stories I've built for myself to reject it, I have felt blessing and adoration my entire life. I've worked for much of it, but never all that hard, and still good things come. Most of the time I feel as though I don't deserve any of it. And that's just in my own skin and with my own family and ordinary life stuff, never mind me trying to make room for the sensation of being adopted into the family of God.

I have not wanted to live up to the potential others see. I have fled to faraway lands. I have sabotaged my life in various ways. I have not wanted to live up to the potential I see, even for the sake of getting what I really want.

I think I'm afraid to live up to my potential, to really risk putting myself out there, because I believe in karma more than I believe in a God who loves me. If I allow myself good things, I am afraid the bad stuff will follow. I drive the good away to try to control how much bad stuff will be mine.

I care more about the sense of control I feel when I think I'm manipulating the way the world works than I care for my Father.

I ... don't ... want ... to ... choose ... God.

So I ask for my inheritance and ignore the Father who gives it.

And he gives it. I sit with it. I see where it could take me. Then, without really thinking about it, I hit the road.

And because I believe in karma and some idea that every good thing must be balanced out with some bad thing, I make sure to ruin my gifts on "wild living," and I limp home again. And again. And again.

THE PRODIGAL'S DILEMMA

I keep repeating the cycle because I refuse to admit what it means to have my Father run to greet me and welcome me home. I have not earned his love and ready response. And my making it more expensive by being a bigger jerk in my behavior and my ingratitude isn't slowing him down as he runs toward me again, and again ... and again. I have not earned his love. I have not spoiled his love. I don't know what to make of the fact that I seem unable to change or diminish his love at all. Part of me wants to have the impervious nature of God's love mean that I don't matter, that his love isn't about me, and that his love is only a reflection of who he is, with no regard to my being a worthy recipient of his love. But then I feel his love and know he sees me quite specifically, and I have to confess that I know his love is very much about me.

The other part of me wants to have my Father's consistent love, and the freedom he gives me to take it or leave it, mean something true and lasting about the reality of life, and about just how right it is that he would love me in such a fashion. I want the consistent and voluntary loving relationship to mean that God wants me enough that he wants me to choose him — that his love is very much about me and what I bring to the relationship. The hope that I could be desirable to God, that somehow I have that sort of value in his eyes, is often too much for me. There is too much potential in that. Too much risk. Too much to live into. Too much putting myself out there. When I get a glimpse of God's generous love, and the choices I have about how I can respond, I find myself feeling a lot like the prodigal son with the full inheritance lavished upon me. It's too much intimacy, too much vulnerability on the part of my Father, and I run from it.

But when I run, it's like there is this magic line I cross. When I cross beyond it, I feel bad. When I come back, I feel God and goodness rush upon me. I've crossed over the line enough times that I'm starting to trust that it's actually real. And the more real it feels, the less desire I have to cross back away from the love. Yet I still cross it. I still fight against giving up control over my Father's love for me. But I am starting to see that this particular way of testing his love has pretty much been tested all it needs to be tested, and neither the line nor the results are going to change.

I was thinking about my testing and my line crossing the day I came across Psalm 16:6. "The boundary lines have fallen for me in pleasant places; surely I have a delightful inheritance."

I think I'm starting to understand something, prodigal that I am, about boundaries and real inheritance. About the love of the Father. About my dad.

We live in a time and a place where freedom is all about how far a person can roam, and for most of my life I've bought into that way of seeing things. Boundaries are fences to keep me in. To hold me back. To control me. To rail against, to test, to probe, to bend, to sneak through to places that feel exotic because they're "other."

But what I'm beginning to see is that my boundaries, my limitations, don't work that way. If the younger brother asks his father for his inheritance early, it will be given. If I reject my dad and stomp off, he'll let me. The boundaries are not prison walls. The boundaries are not restrictions at all. I am still my Father's son even when I am in the faraway land. He will celebrate my return, and there will be more for me on that day. A real boundary is simply the place where my Father will stop because he honors who I am and the freedom I demand, and where he will stand and wait, longingly, for my return.

I have not earned that sort of adoration. Devotion like that has been mostly wasted on me. But something about the fact that my Father is always there waiting for me as I drag my wandering, fearful self home is having an effect on me. He waits for me at the boundaries of the places I have called his. My Father has given me all the domain I have claimed as my own.

I guess that brings up some questions about just who is made free, and who is made captive, by the boundaries in my sinner's heart.

The boundary lines have fallen for me in pleasant places. They have fallen as near to me as I will allow my Father to come. My distance from my Father is the distance I have traveled beyond the place where I told him to stop following me.

Rest from My Enemies

What about the other part of that passage? The part that says surely I have a delightful inheritance. If you trace the ways inheritance is talked about in the Bible, you'll see how it has to do with evidence of God's favor. You'll see rules about how land is to be handed down from generation to generation. You'll see issues of birthright. You'll see Israel described as God's inheritance. You'll also see commands to leave no living thing as God's Promised Land is conquered — no compromise and no gods but the Lord as we follow him. There's a ton of love to be explored in each of those things. After looking at all of that, though, what I think inheritance really comes down to is something like how it's described in Deuteronomy 12:10: "But you will cross the Jordan and settle in the land the Lord your God is giving you as an inheritance, and he will give you rest from all your enemies around you so that you will live in safety."

The enemies will still be around. My enemies will still be around. Papa John's will still run commercials at dinnertime. Family systems will still create frustrations. Fathers will still confuse sons, and sons will still give in to their neuroses and pain. But there is a place of rest. Of safety.

I want that. I want a God who carves out a safe and restful place for me even as I live surrounded by threats and enemies who would seek my destruction.

What's more, I want a God who will let me wander out beyond

my safe place even if I really nail him on the way out. I want a Father who will love me like that, and who will stand at the edge of that safe land. One who will not belittle me by turning that journey into a simple case of make-believe, but who will really let the dogs bite and the bees sting and who will leave me there just as long as I choose. And one who, when I return, will run to greet me, even if his love and delight are adoration and accolade I haven't earned.

To accept his love is to give up control to his unruly love. It means letting him deal with the opinions of other people when I'm celebrated by the God who knows better, and who knows all about me, and who still wants to celebrate my arrival.

Boundaries. Inheritance. Freedom. Love that waits and celebrates the return of a prodigal son. All is evidence of a Father's passion to have his foolish child come to believe the words, "Sweetheart, all I want is to share this life with you."

DISCUSSION QUESTIONS

1. What do you think of the idea that perhaps the Prodigal didn't start out with any intention to leave?

2. In what ways have you been blessed, and then wandered to far-off lands without a plan to do so?

3. How do you feel about the blessings that your Father gives you?

4. What have you been taught about the strings that come attached to God's gifts?

5. *The boundary lines have fallen for me in pleasant places.* How have you experienced God's boundary lines in your life? How have they felt pleasant to you?

6. What would you lose if you chose to stay at home with the Father?

CHAPTER 11

THE PROSTITUTE:
WHY IS ANYTHING SOFT?

I bet I hear four or five sermons about prostitutes every year. Always about women or young children. And I'm tired of prostitute stories about women and how somebody finds the courage to love a prostitute in spite of how they've made their money. There are too many oppressive circumstances in life that drive women and children to that end. Those are not the sort of whores I see the Bible wagging a finger at. The Bible expresses an understanding of a simple truth that our victim-blaming illustrations tend to ignore: most prostitutes find their way to their profession as a matter of survival. It's a lousy thing when the world crushes a person, ignores them, and then calls them names when they make the horrifying choices left to them by our unjust apathy. The world won't be made stronger by having me add to that pile.

Besides, the bulk of the real whores in the world are men.

WHORES WITHOUT A FIGHT

Most of the whorish choices any of us make come easily, from greed or convenience or lack of character. And these choices are almost always made when there are not only plenty of other options, there are plenty of better options.

We're whores because we're fools, not because we're oppressed. And we're whores because we don't even think to ask what access to our truly intimate places means, let alone what it is worth.

We get stuck in our whorish ways after they become our normal way of thinking, after we have allowed them to define us. We understand ourselves as whores after we have become slaves. No surprise there. That's what addiction, sin, and a failure look like. And by the time we're slaves, we're tragedies, to be lumped in with the oppressed others who normally shape the anecdotes and cautionary tales of morality and intimacy sold cheap. But there is a time when a besetting sin is still merely an *on*-setting sin, before its hold has won out, when we can still choose a different way. And if that's true, then the important question becomes: what kind of fool falls for the whore's lifestyle in the first place?

King Ahab, the great whore of the Old Testament, chose a life of idolatry and villainy because he lost touch with God and with the promises that came to Ahab through generations of God's people. Ahab lost his grip on the truth, and the Bible calls him a whore for the comforts he chased instead of God.

Ahab said to Elijah, "So you have found me, my enemy!"

"I have found you," he answered, "because you have sold yourself to do evil in the eyes of the Lord. He says, 'I am going to bring disaster on you. I will wipe out your descendants and cut off from Ahab every last male in Israel — slave or free. I will make your house like that of Jeroboam son of Nebat and that of Baasha son of Ahijah, because you have aroused my anger and have caused Israel to sin.'

"And also concerning Jezebel the Lord says: 'Dogs will devour Jezebel by the wall of Jezreel.'

"Dogs will eat those belonging to Ahab who die in the city, and the birds will feed on those who die in the country."

1 KINGS 21:20 – 26

Where do I lose my grip on something true? What lies do I tend to believe instead? Where do I get fooled?

What about the Church?

And Christians?

And you?

My belief is that fools are fools because they refuse to believe God when he says, "Sweetheart, all I want is to share this life with you." Some other voice insists that can't be true, and a fool believes the wrong voice.

"Sweetheart, all I want is to share this life with you."

With us.

Sharing *life* with us, we sweethearts.

All the Father wants ...

The word is *communion*. From the Latin for "state of belonging equally to, or shared equally by, two or more parties." Your life — and God's life   belonging equally to, and shared equally by, you and God. This is all he wants.

I say the deal favors us. But God's the one who carries it as his deep, deep yearning. All the Father wants is to commune with you, to share this life with you.

Is that what you've been taught? Does it feel too simple? Like maybe the word *all* is pushing things too far? Do you wonder what Mr. Know-It-All, the annoying guy in your small group, would say about that? Or your pastor?

Here's what I've always heard from people who tell me how to do Christianity: Faith is not supposed to be that easy. Like there's more to it than just communion with the Almighty Maker of the Universe. Like sharing life with God couldn't possibly be enough. Faith is supposed to be harder than that.

The prodigal returns home and his father welcomes him. Welcomes him *home*. The place is his. He has to share it with his family, sure, and with whoever else depends on the place. There is work to be done for and with his father, of course. But the place is his, and there's nothing he needs to do to make that simple truth more true. The communion is established.

The same is true for your Father in heaven. Your Father owns the place and delights in your presence. All that you have is in his name. All that you can contribute with your efforts will be valued only because he loves having you around. It's not the work that matters to him; it's your being with him.

What are you possibly going to add in a material, intellectual, professional, or religious sense to the incalculable riches of your Father?

All you can offer is your company and your attention, your love and your invitation to know and be known, to share your life with your Father who protects you and who loves you, and whose inheritance to you is delightful.

The deal favors you. You delight him.

Israel is God's inheritance. *You* are God's inheritance. Your life and his life are shared equally. Your inheritance is him, and his inheritance is you.

Christians are big on talking about how when you die it all goes back in the box, how we can't take our stuff and our riches with us when we go. Some people also recognize that even our "legacy" — that seductive contemporary lover embraced by a great many whores — doesn't last that long either. Legacies, pursued for the sake of legacy, are investments of rapidly diminishing value in a market that competes with the God who would be our only inheritor, and who will surely be more than adequate as our only inheritance. But maybe that's a side issue for now.

The point people make when they talk about our not being able to take it with us is that we are better off focusing on what will endure, namely our relationship with God. Their point is that our death is the day of our great reward, so we should work for that true treasure. You know what, though? That's also the day of God's great reward, because that's the day we finally put down all the garbage and look to him.

Which brings us back to whores like us, and the institutions and institutional lies that guide us.

Here are truths that whores tend to forget. These truths apply equally well to liaisons in dark alleys, to the deep lies we cling to in the recesses of our minds, to the choices we make and the principles we adopt about employment, to the ways we engage in party politics, to the ways we interact with God, and most certainly to the choices made by churches big and small.

> Whores were created by God, in God's image, and deserve to be approached with reverence.
>
> Whores have a deep desire to be intimately known, and to experience vulnerability in safety.
>
> Vulnerability experienced in hostile or mercenary settings limits a whore's ability to be known intimately in a safe setting, and therefore limits the whore's likelihood of ever satisfying their deep desires.
>
> Whores were created with all of the requisite "equipment" to bridge the distances between us and to receive love in the context of safe vulnerability. No additional tools, techniques, or participants are required.
>
> Whores were born to love, and there is a great cost to their true lover when they erode their ability to love by embracing false lovers.
>
> The value of a whore's love is incalculable — whatever price it may bring on the open market.
>
> When God looks at a whore, he does not see a whore. God sees only someone he insists on referring to as Sweetheart.

LOVERS

You know what? You know all of this already. You've heard it a thousand times.

So why in the world are you reading yet another book about God and his love?

What gives?

Do you get traction with the idea that you long for intimacy and vulnerability in a safe relationship, where you can explore and *be explored*? What do you think of that, you being explored? Augustine called the Father the lover, the Son the beloved, and the Spirit as the searching love that passes between them. If God is your lover, the Holy Spirit is the caress, the tickle, the intimate touch that arouses the passions.

Is that too creepy for you? Thinking of God touching your skin? Thinking of an intimacy akin to sexual intimacy?

Language about prostitutes I can handle. I can work with the prostitute metaphor. I'm used to hearing that one. But the God whose fingers drag across my chest? Too much. That sort of intimacy mixes types of love, after all. You know, God's love is *agape* love, brotherly love is *phileo* love, and sexual love is *eros* love. Remember the four dozen sermons you've heard about that? God does only the first one, because he's perfect. The others don't translate.

There is this, though: Jesus had brothers and disciples. He knows *phileo* love. Jesus is fully man just as he is fully divine. If you're going to give him *agape and phileo*, you gotta give him some *eros*.

I'm not talking about praying for some sexual encounter with God, by the way. I'm talking about opening yourself up to be loved in ways that you can understand and that can mean something to your gut. The fact that our discomfort with sexuality inhibits our ability to allow God into our lives is just lame.

I mean, how much more intimate is the searching love of God than the touch of a human lover? How much more vulnerable? How much more profoundly naked? How much more gratifying? How much more delightfully captivating?

God is not some parent asleep upstairs while the kids mess around on the sofa of Earth. God is not some taskmaster who only shows up to pass out the scores. God is not Santa Claus, watching you while you sleep and leaving presents if you can trick him into it by being mostly good for the few days before Christmas.

God is the only lover who will satisfy the portions of your soul that were meant to be known only by God. Think tender kisses. Think sun-dappled afternoons on the sofa. Think winks and grins. Think questions about what it's like to be you. Think roadside assistance and perfect attendance at recitals. Think the robe sliding off your shoulders to the floor and this moment of surreal vulnerability. Think of God looking straight at you and sighing "Wow."

If you don't get naked with God, you will sneak your validation elsewhere. You were born a lover, born to give love and to receive love. You *will* seek to have your needs met. And that is a very, very good thing about you.

Who loves you now? With whom are you most yourself? With whom do you feel most valuable?

Where do you love now? Where are you most naked? Where do you risk what matters to you?

Here's a word for you: *cathexis*. It's a Freudian term that has to do with the investment of libidinal, or worship-deep, energy into a person, object, organization, or concept. Cathexis is what makes heirlooms so precious. Cathexis inspires song lyrics like "I can't live, if living is without you-u-u ..." Cathexis is what turns believers into zealots, worshipers into terrorists, and patriotism into white-cowboy-hat-wearing invasion forces. It's what builds idols and religions, heroes and canonized saints. Cathetic devotion to specific verses-turned-doctrine is what gave rise to the Inquisition, and to Evangelicalism.

Cathexis is what whores get instead of love.

Here's another word: *affexis*. I made it up. Rooted in the word "affection," affexis is the strong bonding energy between two or more mutually attractive and attracted persons who are then engaged in mutual yet utterly unselfish delight. Affexis heralds a shift from "God's will" to Jesus' "wanna?"

Cathexis says influence equals leadership. Affexis insists that leadership is measured by the communion facilitated between the follower and the Father.

Cathexis requires answers. Affexis needs only relationship with the Father.

Cathexis builds systematic theologies and governs with cumbersome principles. Affexis looks to the joyful cloud of witnesses from Hebrews 12, hears our friend Paul say, "Follow [me] as I follow … Christ" (1 Corinthians 11:1), and grins when Jesus says, "I am the way and the truth and the life. No one comes to the Father except through me" (John 14:6).

Cathexis seeks to create proxies, structures, and filters. Affexis offers introductions.

Cathexis strokes its beard and weighs value. Affexis is an usher's sweeping gesture to the Throne.

Cathexis sells remedies. Affexis invites suffering people into the cure.

Cathexis is the reason you are still reading books on God's love. Affexis is the craving for love that has kept you from putting the books down.

You know, at a level that is deeper down than any sermon or any stupid book on God's love can ever reach, right where the robe rests on your shoulder. You know that you will hear the "wow." You know that the idols have gotten in your way, have not been safe, have been a lousy intimate trade because they have not borne the sacred image you bear, and aren't even what you really want.

Please, just for now, stop reading.

Pray yourself dropping the robe.

DISCUSSION QUESTIONS

1. Where have you grown accustomed to playing the role of whore in your world?

2. *Communion: the state of belonging equally to, or shared equally by, two or more parties. Your life and God's life belong equally to, and are shared equally by, you and God. This is all he wants.* What do you think of that? What would that look like in your world on a bad day?

3. What about your body would God notice when you dropped the robe? Where do you most crave his approval of your body?

4. How does sexual union relate to communion with God?

5. How does orgasm relate to ecstatic experiences in worship or prayer?

CHAPTER 12

The Failure:
Prophets and Track Shoes

So you drop the robe. You stand naked before God. You hear him breathe his appreciative and grateful "Wow." Communion is established. You feel him enter your life, and you feel the invitation into his. You feel yourself invited to play wherever you choose. You come to see that the only boundaries between you and God are the places where you tell him to stop following you. You cross into communion with him and return home to find joy in being there. You like it. Life opens up to you, and darkness falls away.

POWER

Then God tells you to take a message to King Ahab, the great whore in the palace, or at the family table, or in your circle of friends, or in your church, or, far more likely, in your own heart. We all have jabbering fiends and King Ahabs ruling in monstrously violent and idolatrous ways in our hearts. The God who loves you and who offers you his life also claims your life, and he isn't a big fan of King Ahab's leadership style.

> Now Elijah the Tishbite, from Tishbe in Gilead, said to Ahab, "As the Lord, the God of Israel, lives, whom I serve, there will be neither dew nor rain in the next few years except at my word."
>
> Then the word of the Lord came to Elijah: "Leave here, turn eastward and hide in the Kerith Ravine, east of the Jordan. You will drink from the brook, and I have directed the ravens to supply you with food there."
>
> So he did what the Lord had told him. He went to the Kerith Ravine, east of the Jordan, and stayed there. The ravens brought him bread and meat in the morning and bread and meat in the evening, and he drank from the brook.
>
> 1 KINGS 17:1 – 6

Elijah said many things in his life before he shows up in God's Word, but he doesn't show up in God's Word until he speaks from his shared life with God and tells the whore King Ahab how things are going to be, and by whose power. First Kings 17:1 says, "Now Elijah the Tishbite, from Tishbe in Gilead, said to Ahab, 'As the Lord, the God of Israel, lives, whom I serve, there will be neither dew nor rain in the next few years except at my word.'"

I said a great many things in my life before I spoke to the whorish king inside of me, but I had no voice to do so until I spoke from my shared life with God. Then I told my addictions how things are going to be, and by whose power.

A little over a year ago, I asked God to take my difficulties, my addictions, from me, that victory over them may bear witness to those I would help of his power, his love, and his way of life.

WEAKNESS

The next verses in the Elijah story are, "Then the word of the Lord came to Elijah: 'Leave here, turn eastward and hide in the Kerith Ravine, east of the Jordan. You will drink from the brook, and I have directed the ravens to supply you with food there.' So he did what the Lord had told him. He went to the Kerith Ravine, east of the Jordan, and stayed there. The ravens brought him bread and meat in the morning and bread and meat in the evening, and he drank from the brook."

You've dropped the robe. You've heard the "wow." You've engaged the living communion. You are led to your King Ahab to make your bold proclamation. And then you're told to run away and hide.

Say *what?*

Being right, or speaking from your shared life with God, doesn't mean you get to stand there and wait for the ring announcer to show up and strap the big gold boxing championship belt around your waist. Being right and obeying God doesn't mean that the person you speak to will drop to their knees and repent or change their ways and give up their idols or the idolatrous roles they've played in your world.

I can tell you that the King Ahab of Stuffed Crust Pizza doesn't give up without a fight. We live in the kingdom of Ahab, and while there is no question that the Earth is God's footstool and that he owns the cattle on a thousand hills and that nothing can separate us from the love of Christ Jesus, don't let yourself believe the bad guys are so obviously bad that God's not treating them with the same love and patience he uses on you when you're the prodigal. Ours is not a battle of power; it is an engagement of love by the One who is Truth. In other words, if you're going to speak for the God whose love will pass through you to reach others, in your heart or in your world, tie your shoelaces first.

Imagine what it was like to be Elijah. At first you were just some guy. Then you have this experience with God. And the relationship grows. There are ups and downs as you develop your response time to his voice. Then you're led to the king, whose practices have been disgusting and confusing to you but to whom you long to feel honor and trust, because he is the king, after all — and God tells you to speak.

That day with the king was a pretty big one for Elijah. A long time coming, and pretty heady stuff, speaking to the king on behalf of God. And then for it to be a real doozy of a "thus sayeth the Lord" smackdown too. How much adrenaline must Elijah have felt that day? That's like break-a-brick-with-your-head-ninja-style awesome.

Until God says to get the heck out of Dodge.

That can't be what Elijah was hoping his career as prophet was going to look like.

OBEDIENCE

I guess the question is this: Are we to measure our success with God by outcomes or by obedience?

It doesn't take a genius to know that obedience is the right answer, but it's worth noting what would have happened to Elijah if he had gotten stuck focusing on the outcomes, namely the response from Ahab, instead of being singularly focused on obedience to God. The king's repentance could have made a huge difference in the lives of a great many people who were going to be impacted by a drought and resulting famine. Had Elijah ignored God's order to flee, if Elijah had gotten confused about whether outcomes or obedience were the important thing, he would have been killed by Ahab.

Anyone who has ever fought against an addiction or deep sin knows that all you really do when you turn to face the monster is get it to turn to face you. If you don't have ways to keep you from having to go toe to toe, strength on strength against your giant — as David had his sling and five smooth stones when he stepped out to face Goliath — it is no surprise when the evil spirit returns to you and brings seven spirits more wicked than itself along as roommates.

If Elijah had been more focused on outcomes than obedience, he may well have been confused or frightened to distraction by God's word for him to flee, and he would have lost his sense of grounding and peace with God.

If he had done that, the voice of The Failure would have jumped in.

Hotshot prophet delivers hotshot news to king. Last seen fleeing town in tears. Many seen pointing and laughing.

Fat guy gets serious about kicking food addiction and tells family he can't eat what they're eating at Christmas dinner. Family smirks and mutters that this diet will fail too.

Pastor preaches on purity of heart. Last seen installing accountability software to keep him from surfing porn. Congregation and outsiders call him hypocrite.

It's a hard thing to play the part of prophet, even in your own heart. It's scary and lonely, and the soundtrack from the *Rocky* movies doesn't follow you around to keep you pumped. I get why Elisha would call bears from the woods to maul forty-two kids who made fun of his haircut. Jeering from the crowd is sometimes more than a person can take — or should have to.

> From there Elisha went up to Bethel. As he was walking along the road, some boys came out of the town and jeered at him. "Get out of here, baldy!" they said. "Get out of here, baldy!" He turned around, looked at them and called down a curse on them in the name of the Lord. Then two bears came out of the woods and mauled forty-two of the boys. And he went on to Mount Carmel and from there returned to Samaria.
>
> 2 KINGS 2:23 – 25

And while I'm mentioning Elisha and the forty-two, I'd like to point out that even though obedience may come with track shoes, sometimes God does bring the hammer on behalf of those whose lives are entwined with his own.

We live in a time when comedians live on asides and undermining punch lines, when sound bites on news channels are paired out of context for the sake of presenting sensationalized contradictions and supposed flip-floppery, and when we race from one quick fix to another because our fad-driven culture insists that the only good way to lose 200 pounds is to lose it sometime during the half-hour radical makeover show. This sort of rigid demand for immediate gratification forces our hands, forces militant win-lose power plays at home, in the public square, and in our own hearts, and forces faith to forego love for prodigals and whorish kings. Meanwhile, it slaps the label of *failure* on followers who actually lace up when God tells them to hit the road for whichever Kerith Ravine may be home to God's bread-bearing ravens.

Tell me, would you rather be a servant to your King Ahab, or would you rather experience the ridiculous miracle of being fed twice daily by birds made obedient by the love of God Almighty?

POWER IN WEAKNESS

It's July 7, 2007. I'm driving from Franklin, Tennessee, on my way home to Indianapolis. I'd spoken at a prison outside of Nashville, spent several days with friends, signed with a manager, and made contact with a couple of prospective copywriting clients. And I'd made it through the long weekend without eating too much or eating any of the wrong stuff. It was a heady time for me. There were new dreams of pursuing my passion as my career.

And then it occurred to me: I was hungry and I didn't know what I was going to do for food. Drive-through options were out, and I sure didn't want to eat at a gas station. I also didn't want to make a big deal out of finding food. It wasn't like I was going to gorge myself. It was more that everything else had gone so perfectly, and I didn't want to have to make room in my joy for a compromised choice, you know?

So I prayed. I told God that I loved doing this new way of life with him. I told him I was afraid of making a poor choice with my meal. I thanked him for wanting to be involved in such mundane moments as my meals. Then I told him that if the next exit, which was still a few miles ahead, only had fast food, I was going to get that and I wasn't going to mess with guilt about it. I told him that if I could have any food, I would choose some green grapes, some cashews, a little brie, and a bottle of water. I said "amen" and waited to see what would happen. I figured I was mostly just playing a little game of rationalization with myself before I ended up at Taco Bell.

The green highway signs came into view, announcing the exit's offerings. The sign listing the gasoline options included Kroger gas. Kroger, as in the grocery store. I pounded on the ceiling and yelled about how awesome God is. I exited. I bought green grapes, some cashews, a little brie, and a bottle of ice cold water.

It was the best meal I've ever had.

It was as though God was saying, "Sweetheart, all I want is to share this life with you."

I guarantee bread and meat delivered by ravens is just as good.

And you don't get fed until you flee.

And you don't flee until you speak.

And you don't speak until you drop the robe.

And a person who wakes sleeping giants, who prophesies to whorish kings in God's name and at God's urging, and who obeys God in flight to a place of God's protection and provision — that person is anything, *anything* but a failure.

DISCUSSION QUESTIONS

1. What is the "King Ahab" in your world?

2. Describe the scene in which you speak God's truth to your King Ahab. What does the room or space look like? What are you each wearing? If you sit with the scene, can you find Jesus there with you? To whom is Jesus turned, and what can you read in his body language? Speak. What words come? How does your voice sound?

3. Where in your world do you go for comfort and protection from God as you obey and face the wrath of your King Ahab?

4. How does God take care of you in your struggle?

CHAPTER 13

The Priest:
Little Do We Know

My mom called a few weeks ago. She hadn't read the early chapters in this book yet, but she had seen my father after he read them.

"Your dad's really hurting right now," she said. "You have to stop this."

"What do you mean?" I knew what she meant. Mom is the thermostat in the family. If things get too warm, she cools them off. If relationships cool down, she brings people together again. It's not an uncommon role for the person who builds and protects the nest.

Or for pastors who build safe places for congregations.

"He read what you sent him, and when he came up from the basement, he looked stricken. I asked him what was wrong, and he just muttered, 'I never knew I was such a horrible father.' Pete, you can't keep doing this to him."

It was a lousy, sick-to-my-stomach sort of feeling to hear her say all that.

Moms and Priests

My mother has been the go-between for my dad and me for most of my life. I think he and I have been confused about how to communicate, and maybe Mom's need for us to understand each other has been greater than our own, so we've let her translate. When I was young and felt I wasn't being treated fairly, or when I felt misunderstood, or when I was angry about any number of things about my dad's work life, I would tell my mother. She would explain things to me.

And she would explain things about me to him.

For example, I used to teach our dogs to respond to different words. Otto knew that he was a palindrome, a word spelled the same backwards as forwards, and he would wiggle and jump on me when I'd ask, "Otto, are you a palindrome?" Another dog knew that he was brown, and that his favorite color was purple. He'd wag his tail when I'd ask, "Zildjian, are you blue?" It would wag faster when I'd ask, "Zildjian, are you green?" And when I finally got to "Zildjian, are you brown?" he'd go nuts and we'd wrestle. Same with his favorite color being purple.

One time my mom told me that Dad had asked her, "Why does Pete teach the dogs such weird things?" She said she'd explained that it was just something I liked to do.

I don't know why he didn't ask me himself. Habit, I guess.

The conversations I've had with my dad about the content in this book are the first here's-the-real-me, how-does-the-real-you-feel-about-this? talks we've ever had. They've been frightening. There have been moments when I felt the whole relationship could blow up. Maybe I assumed that if the relationship blew up, Mom would fix it. She'd explain me to my dad, and him to me, and we'd return to some sort of détente for the sake of her feelings.

My mother has nurtured my brothers and me, and has served us in amazing ways that have always preserved our faith in the safety net of our parents' support as we have ventured into the world. But I would never have come to the conclusion that "the Father's love is far more durable than we've come to believe" if I hadn't pursued my dad directly. I knew that what I was sharing would be hard for him — just as sharing it has been hard for me. Leaving that pain unregulated goes against everything my mother has fought for as a nest builder.

Moms, Priests, and Safety

I was experiencing this amazing, terrifying, exhilarating my-dad-loves-me-very-very-much thing as I slogged through old junk with my father. He keeps bringing up "sweetheart" in our conversations, which makes me feel as though we're not so different after all. As though we may be able to explore something new and wonderful together, with his wisdom and my idealism.

Mom called because she wanted me to stop. I think she was afraid that I'd go too far. I think a lot of people who play the role of thermostat or priest fear "too far." But I'm learning about a Father, and a dad, who will wait longingly for my return while I wander in foolish prodigal ways.

What I'm seeing is that maybe too far is an unrealistic fear. So long as I'm interacting directly with my dad, my love for him will keep me engaged and prevent me from burning the connection or consuming his love too selfishly. I think Mom was afraid that my dad would deliver cruel or relationship-truncating words because of his own demands or sense of justice. I don't think my mom knows that his demands and his sense of justice are nothing compared to his love and his desire to know me.

I think this motherly worry happens with pastors and priests too.

There is something important for people who play the priestly role to learn. You can be the prodigal and return home, or be the elder son and begin to speak honestly with your father, and you can experience the establishment of communion. You can respond to your father's urging for you to speak to the whorish kings in your world, and you can learn to be fed by your father's provision, and you can learn that obedience trumps outcomes because God is just as dedicated to the pursuit of his other children as he is to you. You can invite people onto the father's land and you can serve them there, as a mother or a pastor. But even with all of that being the case, *you are still not the father, and you are still not safe.*

Bruised Reeds

Calling my mother unsafe sounds like a horrible thing to say about her, I know. But I'm starting with her because I want to tell you that it's true of you as well, and it's sure as heck true of me. And unsafe is not the same thing as unimportant, wrong, worthless, or bad.

Bible time. As you read this, ask yourself, "Who is the bruised reed or the smoldering wick?"

> At that time Jesus went through the grainfields on the Sabbath. His disciples were hungry and began to pick some heads of grain and eat them. When the Pharisees saw this, they said to him, "Look! Your disciples are doing what is unlawful on the Sabbath."
>
> He answered, "Haven't you read what David did when he and his companions were hungry? He entered

the house of God, and he and his companions ate the consecrated bread — which was not lawful for them to do, but only for the priests. Or haven't you read in the Law that the priests on Sabbath duty in the temple desecrate the Sabbath and yet are innocent? I tell you that one greater than the temple is here. If you had known what these words mean, 'I desire mercy, not sacrifice,' you would not have condemned the innocent. For the Son of Man is Lord of the Sabbath."

Going on from that place, he went into their synagogue, and a man with a shriveled hand was there. Looking for a reason to accuse Jesus, they asked him, "Is it lawful to heal on the Sabbath?"

He said to them, "If any of you has a sheep and it falls into a pit on the Sabbath, will you not take hold of it and lift it out? How much more valuable is a human being than a sheep! Therefore it is lawful to do good on the Sabbath."

Then he said to the man, "Stretch out your hand." So he stretched it out and it was completely restored, just as sound as the other. But the Pharisees went out and plotted how they might kill Jesus.

Aware of this, Jesus withdrew from that place. A large crowd followed him, and he healed all who were ill. He warned them not to tell others about him. This was to fulfill what was spoken through the prophet Isaiah:

"Here is my servant whom I have chosen, the one I love, in whom I delight; I will put my Spirit on him, and he will proclaim justice to the nations. He will not quarrel or cry out; no one will hear his voice in the streets. A bruised reed he will not break, and a smoldering wick he will not snuff out, till he leads justice to victory. In his name the nations will put their hope."

MATTHEW 12:1–21

This isn't a passage I've heard about very many times; but when I have, the bruised reed has been presented as us — people who have been battered by the world, connecting me with the sick people Jesus heals. And the smoldering wick (or flax, which looks like cotton in the field, and is used to make wicks and linen) is supposed to be my feeble faith. The idea I've been taught is that God will not give up on me and snuff me out for my weak faith. It's always a sort of buck-up-little-camper message.

Do you see that meaning for the reed or wick in this passage, at all?

Take a look at 2 Kings 18:21, or Isaiah 36:6, which both say, "Look, I know you are depending on Egypt, that splintered reed of a staff, which pierces the hands of anyone who leans on it! Such is Pharaoh king of Egypt to all who depend on him."

Try this on: Reeds are hollow tubes, like a straw, and their outer layers are made of smaller straws. If you bruise a reed, the bruised place will be the place where it will splinter later, sort of like if you bend a straw until it creases, it will always "break" at that place when you bend it again. A bruised reed is no good for building or leaning on. It is broken where it is bruised. Leaving a bruised reed alone is leaving a lingering danger around.

A wick that is not snuffed out is a fire hazard. It's unsafe. And if you use the word flax, as in flax in a field, the fire hazard, the danger, is even more pronounced. Bruised reeds and smoldering wicks that are not broken or snuffed out are dangers that are *left dangerous*.

King Ahab still has the power to kill Elijah.

The prodigal can leave and hurt the father again.

The elder son can show up with neurotic conclusions that make the father, and mother, feel lousy and misunderstood.

The Pharisees are left to plot against Jesus. They are bruised reeds who will, in fact, pierce the hands of Christ.

Jesus lets his suffering happen because his objective is loving obedience, to do what he sees the Father doing. And the Father loves his prodigal Pharisees too. Jesus doesn't stay and fight with the Pharisees. He doesn't quarrel or cry out. No one hears his voice in the streets. He doesn't call down angels, or Elisha's bears, even though he is challenged and is plotted against. He performs a miracle and speaks from his relationship with his Father, not unlike Elijah before Ahab. And like Ahab with his false securities — or mothers committed to service as family thermostats, or pastors addicted to playing the part of purveyor of God — the Pharisees miss the miracle for the upset and loss of control they fear in its delivery. They respond defensively, with altruistic arguments, to be sure. They plot against Jesus. And Jesus allows them their prodigal distance from the truth that he is. Mercy pours from him in that moment, as he remains committed to loving obedience, to the proclamation of justice. He withdraws from the encounter to go where the Father leads him. And the Pharisees are *left dangerous.*

That same mercy is extended to us even as we remain lodged in our lies, our addictions, or our idolatry. And it is immediately with us when we choose to be done with such things.

WHICH ARE YOU?

So, which are you? Are you more Pharisee or more sick follower seeking mercy? Mercy is extended to both, but the Pharisees choose not to receive it. To them, their way of doing things is still worth fighting for. They are confident in their knowledge, comforted by the role they play, eager to protect the people and to keep the rude child from going too far in protests to the Father; they are more than a little concerned about keeping the Father — rash and vengeful and pitifully proud — from crushing any who would complain or even seek unfiltered connection with the Big Guy.

Here's a litmus test to determine which character you're most like: Pharisee or broken follower. When you see people you want to see experience God's love asking hard questions from soul-deep places, do you let God give his own direct, unfiltered answers? Or do you find yourself interpreting and repeating old party-line excuses and slogans? Worse yet, do you take the anxiety of their discussion upon yourself, getting worked up and insinuating yourself into the interaction the way my mother does?

Kingdoms are built with the taxes priests charge to translate God to children who fear their Father only because they've been told so much about his perfection that his love seems impossible. Grace will be experienced by those who finally admit that they would rather hear of mercy than of kingdoms.

We all play the holy role of priest, in the sense that we are witnesses of God, but we can choose whether we will be the Pharisees who ultimately splinter, fail, and betray. Will we fall victim to our own bruised places, and choose from brokenness and lingering threat, or will we be among the broken and ill who follow Jesus and are healed by him, offering encouragement to others and urging direct interaction with Jesus? Part of the joy of this life on the Father's land, this land of the living, is found in the role of broken encourager. What do we tell the elder brother about his fears and his hurts? What do we tell the prodigal as his eyes start showing that faraway look again?

Do we understand that we are always going to be bruised reeds, no matter what other experiences we may have, and that we will always represent a threat to others?

We are not safe until we come to see that we are terminally *un*safe.

They say that the fear of God is the beginning of wisdom. A fool loses sight of the fact that we are a lingering danger, a reed that will pierce innocent hands, a flame that could send the whole place up in flames, and that we have every reason to fear.

It's terrifying to see what lingering dangers we are. And it's bad news before it is good news.

RECOVERY

God isn't zapping me to benign Zen-like skinniness and interpersonal guru status. This journey has been slow and painful, and the outcome is far from certain. It's been over a year since I started dedicating what is now over fifteen hours per week to recovery in the form of counseling, meetings, study, and exercise — not to mention eating plans and what seems like an ever-expanding list of foods that I'm learning I need to avoid.

I began the recovery work because my wife was at the end of her patience. You can fill in the blanks about the pain and the sorts of conversations and fights we've had. She said I was not emotionally available, that I was gone in my addiction. She was ready to call it quits unless I got serious about turning things around. She delivered the Elijah talk to my Ahab, as it were. She proclaimed that there would be no rain and no dew, or pregnancy due date, so long as I continued in my sin. And once she said what she needed to say in obedience to God, she had to take her hands off the steering wheel and leave the outcome up to me.

It was the bravest thing I've ever been around. It hurt like I'd never felt pain, and it seared my pride to have my wife choose my God over my idols. There was a shrieking inside of me, a horrible moment of crisis. But she had me dead to rights. She was speaking God's words, and I thank him for the way he worked with her to block my escape. All I could do was break. A piece of me died. And a piece of me was brought out of the waters to life.

I am responding. I am earning my wife's trust by living amends to her, and I am becoming safe to her exactly because I live with a growing awareness of just how *un*safe I am to her. Our relationship is richer and more exciting than it's ever been. I think kids will be coming before long, but we both know that I'm a bruised reed and that my only real hope is to continually fall to my God and ask for his mercy and his love as he rearranges the furniture in my soul.

We don't know if I will end up being a story of redemption, or slow tragedy, in my wife's life. We simply do not know. And while that makes me feel small and vulnerable, I wish I could express how good it feels to admit my brokenness and to have God mingle his life with mine, and to have an understanding in my marriage that goes something like: "I ate foolishly today. I am a compulsive overeater, and that's what compulsive overeaters do sometimes."

"I gave in to my fear today, and I didn't come through for you. I'm weak, and that's what weak people do sometimes."

I looked to you to be my comfort and my security, and I chose you over God. I'm an idolater, and that's what idolaters do sometimes.

I got between you and your father today, and I cost you the chance to know each other better. I'm your mother, and that's what mothers do sometimes.

Oh, God, I chose life beyond the boundary where I told you to stop following me. I am a prodigal who struggles to believe that you really love me as you say you do, and that's what prodigals do sometimes.

Father, I was afraid to tell you what I was feeling and thinking. I turned you into a monster in my thoughts. I am an elder brother, and that's what elder brothers do sometimes.

Jesus, I saw your miracle today, but I sought to silence you because if you are who you say you are, that changes everything for me. I am a priest who loves your people on my terms instead of yours, and that's what priests do sometimes.

Lord, we are reeds who have been bruised so that we might experience the joy of your mercy, but we are so afraid of falling upon your mercy. We are sinners, and that is what we do sometimes.

I am so, so tired, Lord. I want to come home. I want to tell you what I have felt about you and have shared with anyone but you concerning how I see you. I want to hear your voice. I want to speak from my relationship with you. I want to experience your provision. I want to see what my life looks like if I linger in Good Friday and let you change me. Is that still even possible? Are you real that way?

You already know what he says.

Sweetheart, all I want is to share this life with you.

Discussion Questions

1. Who are the "thermostats" in your world? The people who cool relationships down when people get frustrated, and who bring people together when relationships cool too far.

2. How do you feel about those thermostats or priests? How do words like *gratitude, manipulation, obligation, guilt, invasion, stuck, love, inspiration, safety,* and *proper* stir into those feelings?

3. How do you feel about the idea that you are *unsafe,* and that you are *left dangerous*? Does that feel more like good news or bad news?

4. How can you be unsafe, part of a royal priesthood of believers, a sinner, and a saint all at the same time?

PART V

CRYING OUT

CHAPTER 14

A Son, and Nothing More

We forget love and immediately become tyrants, slaves, or fools when we believe God wants us to be more than his children; when we forget that we are adequate in our Father's eyes exactly as we are, that our voices matter to him, and that he wants nothing more than to share life with us. The problem is not our failures or our lack of understanding or our lack of maturity. The problem is that we forget that we were never intended to live without God, beyond utter dependence upon him.

When I was a kid, I once read about President William Taft being buried in a coffin the size of a piano box. He was that big. That remains the main thing I remember about the man.

I've been terrified about the prospect of ending up in an oversized coffin ever since. I mean, it's one thing to live a life that others call misguided or foolishly self-destructive, but so long as I'm alive, there is still the chance that I can change. If I die and am buried in a coffin the size of a piano box, my family and friends will not only have to deal with normal grief, they'll have to find a place for the anger they'll feel about the foolish choices that will have led to my early demise. If I die from my sin, the shame becomes truly permanent. My life would be summed up as a tragedy of selfishness and gluttonous stupidity, a tribute to the choices I made to comfort myself rather than honoring the people whose lives were entwined with my own.

I don't want to poison my family's memory of me with anger, and I am horrified that I could do just that.

Ah, right there — the whorish lure of legacy-building. It's not the hurting of my family that troubles me, it's my legacy, the fact that I would never be able to correct my errors. I would be buried in shame. I care more about my reputation than I care about the people who love me.

I am a bruised reed. A lingering threat.

Legacies are not intended to be the pursuit of sons.

Back to my horror about my sins. I'm only truly horrified when my sense of responsibility insists that it is up to me to fix things. Only when I believe that I made the bed and now I have to lie in it. Only when I believe that I dug myself into this mess, so now I have to dig myself out. Only when I believe that the issue is the result of a lack of discipline that I can somehow turn around if I gain a little more knowledge, a little more resolve, and a little more toughness. I panic when I find myself alone with my sin and the future it holds for me.

Part of what makes the shame so monstrous is my sense that the buck stops with me, and that the only chance I have for recovery is found in some miraculous change of personal strength. I have no credibility with myself in the areas I've spent years trying to discipline only to fail there over and over again. I have completely stripped the gears in that part of my soul, and when I find myself trying to muster the "venture capital" for yet another diet or tough and disciplined approach to the problem, I quickly find that I am no longer at all "bankable." I simply do not believe myself when I promise to make it better, to change my ways, or to stick to the new program.

A coffin the size of a piano box.

I am powerless to escape that hateful destination.

Powerless

We all face hateful destinations that we are powerless to escape.

This is true of individuals, and it's certainly true of organizations.

The first step is admitting powerlessness. It's big and scary and feels a lot like giving up, but it is terrifically good news, and ultimately — ironically — it's the only way to escape despair.

Admitting powerlessness is anything but adopting passivity. It's been said that evangelicals are not only saved by grace, they're paralyzed by it. All too often life is squandered on a silly passivity that indolently waits for God to zap the problem and make things better. This isn't faith. This is magic. It is also the complete abdication of both our humanity and our confession of the reality of God. God offers us communion — an equal sharing and ownership — of our life and his. He is our strong tower, our place of refuge. But he is not our cop-out. Thank him for that, because so long as you experience the pain and slog your way through the healing, which happens under his protection, you are afforded life and reality and can finally be done with the false constructs of deeply held neuroses.

What's news to me is that powerlessness is not the same thing as failure, or at least that failure is not the same thing as shame. Recognizing powerless is a lot like the moment when God asked Adam and Eve, "Who told you that you were naked?" They hadn't been blind previously; it's just that previously their nakedness had never been cause for shame and hiding. Admitting powerlessness to God is a lot like stepping out from the fig leaves.

COMMUNION

But I've not been one to step boldly from my hiding place. That's not the sort of approach to life that I've adopted over the years. I don't know what other people were trying to teach me, but I know that what I learned was something that felt more like, "[Now since you have become] partakers of the divine nature," dear readers of 2 Peter 1, "applying all diligence, in your faith supply moral excellence, and in your moral excellence, knowledge, and in your knowledge, self-control, and in your self-control, perseverance, and in your persever-ance, godliness, and in your godliness, brotherly kindness, and in your brotherly kindness, love" (vv. 4–7 NASB).

I saw passages like that, trimmed out like that, and I thought, "Well, I guess that's the way it is. It looks like I need to start working harder at doing the prescribed things to be a good Christian." I felt as though I needed to prove that I was a "partaker of the divine nature," even though I knew I was still just a guy with ordinary problems and the same need for the Cross I'd ever had.

Does your gut — never mind your faith or your doctrine, be-cause it's more than just the Church that teaches us about redoubling our efforts and being tough on our weak selves — feel like that to you? Do you look at lists like the one above and see a checklist of dry stuff that ends in a sort of lame Hallmark card payoff? Practical and good for covering your butt, but utterly without joy or fun?

And why, if this God we're supposed to be pursuing *is* love, would love be the *last* item on the list? I think the important thing to consider is what it means to be a "partaker of the divine nature."

For me it comes back to communion again. The "state of belonging equally to, or shared equally by, two or more parties." Your life, and God's life, belonging equally to, and shared equally by, you and God. This is all he wants.

We enter into communion with God when we cry out in our pain, when we sob into the Cross, when we prodigals turn for home, when we elder brothers tell the truth to our Father, when we come to terms with the fact that we are lingering threats, and when we finally admit that we are powerless to avoid the hateful destinations that will be ours without a Savior. And communion is offered to us because the relationship between the Father and the Son in the fellowship of the Spirit is pure love, which extends itself to be known, which searches to know, and which meets weakness with joy for the sake of shared life and love.

Communion happens only so long as we continue to remember our state of powerlessness. Otherwise we turn from God and define ourselves apart from that dependence. We look for marching orders and check boxes and tricks that we believe will impress him later, and we become our own self-defined gods.

It's Okay

When we seek to live as more than children of God, when we fight for control instead of reveling in our loving dependence, we eventually break, and some of us find ourselves dropped into the ground in coffins the size of piano boxes.

The mercy of God is that he has retained exclusive rights to his image, which we bear in our hearts and over which we exercise no final control.

We can sharpen our minds, and we have wisdom that can guide our wills. We have been given a certain influence in those areas. But communion with the Father does not flow from the outside in, whatever inspirational or toxic influences reach us that way. No matter how bravely we may attempt to live otherwise, communion with the Father happens from our hearts, where we are powerless apart from the shared life with God.

You are powerless.

But it's okay; your Father is with you.

You are a son. Or you are a daughter. You are not *a* child, in the sense that you are to remain forever childish; but you are *his* child, in the sense that who you are and what you mean and what life is about is derived from your relationship with your Father. And this life is not a test, a riddle, something you have to figure out before you reach some age of accountability when you will become the eldest generation. Your heavenly Father will not die, and while he will most certainly cause you to grow, you will never have to learn to do his job.

You can stop doing God's job.

He is real, and all he wants is to share your life with you.

Your job, made easier and secured by the wisdom presented in passages like the one from Peter's second letter, is to invite your Father to be with you.

Discussion Questions

1. What hateful destinations are you powerless to escape?

2. What is the difference between grace and being made adequate by having God give you enough extra credit points?

3. What is the difference between forgiveness and healing?

4. What is the difference between healing and intimacy?

5. What is the difference between brokenness and wholeness?

6. What is the difference between being defined by your function and being defined by relationship?

CHAPTER 15

COMMUNION OF SIBLINGS

My brothers sometimes jokingly call me Wayne, the bullying older brother from the television show *The Wonder Years*. The habit was born back when the show was still on the air, back when we were still living under the same roof, but the reference to Wayne still happens sometimes. It's evidence of old pestering wounds. I know that so long as the jokes continue, so will the unforgiveness — and the stew of miscommunication, fear, and vilification that unforgiveness requires to survive.

I earned their anger. I did lousy things to them, and for whatever positive influence I've had, relationships don't work like an accounting sheet, where losses and gains cancel each other out to give a final tally. I did good things. And I did bad things, and the two stand side by side. It's only a rich man's shame, or an elder son's fear, that keeps a person from recognizing that and interacting with individual experiences and conclusions in a case-by-case, memory-by-memory manner. Who are they to complain about what I did? At least I wasn't as bad as I could have been.

Who are any of us to tell God about what this life has felt like, and what conclusions we've reached, and to admit that we feel as though he's at least partly to blame for it? Maybe we should just leave well enough alone.

BROTHERLY LOVE

I don't believe God means for us to make do with lives made smaller by leaving well enough alone. I don't believe that's how he invites us to interact with him, or how he intends for us to interact with our brothers.

I've started telling my brothers about my experiences with our father and our mother, who tends to play the role of priest. I expected them to respond negatively, because I am messing with the family rules, after all. But that's not what's happening. They're fascinated to hear how our parents, especially our father, have been responding to having me tell them about the painful moments. It's been really cool being able to tell them what a pleasant surprise I've experienced in learning that I am far more loved, exactly as I am, no matter what I bring up, and that our parents love having me in their lives.

It's not that my brothers didn't know that already. But it feels good to truly get to *know* it, deep down and for real.

I believe they are next. It will be their turn with Dad and with Mom next. And with me.

I think it's easier to talk about struggles between siblings than it is to address issues with parents. Siblings share a more common ground and speak a more common language. They have seen the parents from similar perspectives, and they can compare notes.

"When Dad said that thing to you, how did you take it?"

"Can you help me understand why we're just not clicking?"

"Are you sometimes afraid of what Dad will say?"

"I feel like I should major in business, even though I'd rather be a teacher, because he's paying the tuition, and I feel like I should do what brings the best return on his investment."

"I've made that mistake too. Here's where I was wrong."

While it's great to be learning from one another about the Father, what's even better is the chance to enter into the same communion with our siblings as we experience with God. The way in is exactly the same.

"I'm sorry."

"When you did that, it hurt me."

"I'm afraid."

"I love you."

"Will you do this with me?"

"Here's who I *really* am. Can you love me anyway?"

"Hey, you don't have to take all of that on yourself."

"Man, that's not true about who you really are."

"I don't call you Dumbass."

"I don't call you Wayne."

We all know this is about more than what happens in my immediate family. Who and what we are is defined by relationship, not by function.

Our function is defined by the life we share.

DISCUSSION QUESTIONS

1. Whose opinions of you scare you?

2. You're planning a cookout in a park in the mountains. Jesus is going to be there. You'll spend the afternoon and the evening together, hanging out and enjoying the sunshine. Who does Jesus hope you'll invite? Who do you most want to bring?

3. Who is most likely to speak the words of God into your heart?

CHAPTER 16

A Spreading Goodness

So what is the big ribbon that goes on all of this talk? How do we summarize a life shared with God and with one another? If we're defined by relationship and not by function, then what is the driving passion of the relationship?

A spreading goodness. As the Puritan Richard Sibbes wrote, "God delights to communicate and spread his goodness."[4]

Here's how that works, and how we're invited into it. In fact, here's how we're part of it regardless of how we respond to the invitation.

"In the beginning was the Word, and the Word was with God, and the Word was God" (John 1:1). In the very beginning of existence, there is a relationship. The God who created the heavens and the earth in Genesis 1:1 is not a singular person, but a singular relationship. The Trinity. And the Trinity was complete, and full of love, and the Trinity exists and is defined by the shared life within it.

The Trinity was happy, complete, full, in communion. The Trinity, from the very beginning, experiences goodness.

The Trinity created the heavens and the earth. It is a joyful goodness that hovers over the waters and then speaks light into being. Goodness begets goodness, and the Trinity extends the nature of the Trinity into what is created. Creation expands, day by day, and God — the indivisible relationship — sees that it is good.

Then the Trinity says, " 'Let *us* make human beings in *our* image, in *our* likeness ...'

"So God created human beings in his own image, in the image of God he created them; male and female he created them" (Genesis 1:26–27, emphasis added).

We exist because the Trinity delights to spread goodness, because it is the nature of goodness and love to expand, to extend, to take delight in what it encounters. While we may think of love or goodness as being something we reserve, guard, and keep sheltered from the risk of contamination, the truth is that the love of the Father is far more durable than we've come to believe. The love of the Father, of the Trinity, delights in spreading God's goodness.

We may turn to passages about being a people set apart or about pure religion having to do with keeping ourselves from being contaminated by the world, but we are also called light, and salt, and yeast that spread, and we are told, time and again, that the people of God will be a blessing to all of creation. We are set apart and kept pure so that we will find our delight in the embrace of the goodness of the Trinity.

This is also — coolness on top of coolness — the very reason that we experience our failings and our pain. Goodness has spread itself into all things for the sake of drawing all things into a joyous and delightful relationship, or communion, with the source of all joy and goodness that is found in the indivisible relationship of the Trinity.

Full Strength the Whole Way

What's more, the spreading goodness of God does not diminish as it spreads. There is every bit as much delight in the prodigal's first thought about home as there is in the moment his father lifts him and spins him in his welcoming embrace. There is as much goodness and joy in the good deed done by the worst sinner as is found in the sustained obedience of the most wrinkled saint. Goodness is a relational state, a harmonic chord struck with the laughter of the Trinity, whose pronouncement of goodness into the world has not been rescinded. The fall of humanity resulted in a shift to a plan B, if you like, but when an all-powerful, all-loving, all-good God is in the mix, there is no way to say that plan B is somehow less perfect than whatever idea we may have about what was supposed to be plan A. The Word that was with God, and that is God, and that has enfolded us, we people who have been and forever will be his delightful good creation, that God is one happy being.

And if God delights in the relationship of the Trinity, and within the spreading goodness of creation, including the pulse of your own beating heart, who are you to do less than delight in the relationship evident in everything that surrounds you?

You exist to experience the joy and the eternal delight of the goodness of the Lord.

The reality of you, and of me, is that we are living evidence of a loving, satisfied, complete, delighting relationship within the Godhead, within the Trinity, and the Cross of Christ reaches deeper than all sin, than all un-goodness, and spreads goodness everywhere.

Our God is happy. Our God is fully, wholly, cast-your-sins-as-far-from-you-as-the-east-is-from-the-west delighted. And God's delight spreads as he spreads his goodness into all things.

I am loved by my dad, and by my mom, and by my brothers, and by my wife, and by my friends, and by my life, and by the joyous Trinity whose delights are everywhere, and whose invitation to celebrate and find joy in spreading that delightful goodness in the form of love and invitation is my wondrous inheritance.

I am more than okay. So are you.

LOVE IN THE HOUSE OF GALL

It's been eight months since I started writing this book. In a few hours I will meet my dad and my brothers for our recently launched weekly video study and discussion time at my parents' home. Before we started doing the weekly study, the four of us (and when my mom joins us for bits and pieces, the five of us) hadn't been alone together for maybe ten years. I have been amazed to see how much we've changed from the selves we used to be, and how many of my perceptions of my family have become inaccurate as we've all changed.

We're rediscovering each other. The process has been full of adventure and satisfaction. My brothers and I ask my dad questions we never thought to ask when we were younger, and wouldn't have understood back then anyway. We ask about marriage, about dreams, about how he made his choices about money or dreams in light of his marriage and his role as father.

And in these times together, and in the questions about how my dad sees the world, he gets to become our friend. He talks about the mistakes he made, or how he wishes he would have done things differently, and we listen and remember what he tells us. The gap between us is shrinking, and the intimacy between us is growing. That intimacy feels frightening because there is very real power in it. We have a long history together, and it is important that we navigate the relationship with love and care, not because the love is fragile, but because the relationship is exciting and the intimacy is something none of us wants to tax through carelessness.

The relationship I'm experiencing with my dad and brothers, and the ache I have for it to repeat itself with my heavenly Father and my Christian brethren, frequently reminds me of the relationship between Moses and God. I picture the connection between them toward the end of the book of Exodus. Moses develops this friendship, this beautiful sonship, really, with God. God writes the Ten Commandments on two stone slabs, and then Moses gets so angry with the Israelites and their idolatry that he drops the slabs and they shatter. God is furious with the Israelites too. But Moses asks God to show mercy to the Israelites because of the relationship Moses and God have developed. God agrees, and a short time later, God invites Moses to bring two more slabs up the mountain so God can write the Commandments again.

What a beautiful relationship that is. How delicate. Can you imagine the depth of adventure and satisfaction that was blended into it? God seems to take a genuine delight in Moses, and their time together leaves Moses' face radiant.

I think it's cool that people could tell when Moses had spent time with God, but what I'm after is what that radiance felt like on the inside. How much goodness and joy does it take to fill a person up so much that it shows? Just how wonderful must that feel?

THE END

It's been eight months, as I said.

I've lost fifteen pounds, and I have a very long way to go.

I continue with the recovery program. I have hired a personal trainer. I am wearing through shoes on the treadmill at the gym. I am enjoying my time inventing new recipes in the kitchen.

I'm going in the right direction.

But mostly I love, *love*, where I am, and who has come running to meet me here. All I had to do was tell my Father that I was willing to have him come to me. All I had to do was tell my Father that I hurt, and that I wanted to know his presence.

And goodness spread upon me. My delight is in his goodness and in seeing how he has formed me in his image so that his goodness becomes my goodness. It is my delight to spread the goodness further into the world for the sake of the joy set before me.

These, my friend, are the facts of the Lord's spreading goodness within me:

There is so much more than the small life many of us have settled for.

There is meaning and joy and the lightening of a great many loads.

There is peace and there is forgiveness and there is good news yet unheard.

There is communion with the Father, Son, and Spirit, and with the world.

There is love.

DISCUSSION QUESTIONS

1. *We exist because the Trinity delights to spread goodness, because it is the nature of goodness and love to expand, to extend, and to delight in what it encounters.*

   Where in your world do you experience a contented, spreading goodness where you are happy just to be alive?

2. What if you could move from the side of the table where you sit with your sin and your shame to the other side of the table to sit with the Father? What if, looking back from the Father's side of the table, you were able to see your sin and your shame not as reflections of your wickedness, but as the project upon which God takes great delight to work with you? What if your struggles and your junk were a fascinating puzzle to God, and your company as you worked on the puzzle with him was his great joy? Would you want that — to have your heart be God's companion, and your body be the engrossing task to which you both turned your cooperative attention?

3. What if that's already what's happening?

NOTES

1. Will D. Campbell, *Brother to a Dragonfly* (New York: Seabury, 1977), 221f., quoted in Philip Yancey, *What's So Amazing About Grace?* (Grand Rapids: Zondervan, 1997).

2. Martin Luther, in a letter to Melanchthon, August 1, 1521, vol. 48, *Luther's Works*, American Edition, 281–2.

3. Augustine of Hippo, Sermon on 1 John 7, 8 [1] Cf. Augustine on Galatians 6:1: "And if you shout at him, love him inwardly; you may urge, wheedle, rebuke, rage; love, and do whatever you wish. A father after all, doesn't hate his son; and if necessary, a father gives his son a whipping; he inflicts pain, to insure well-being. So that's the meaning of acting in a spirit of mildness (Gal. 6:1)." Sermon 163B:3:1, *The Works of Saint Augustine: A New Translation for the 21st Century* (Sermons 148–153), 1992, part 3, vol. 5, 182.

4. "The Successful Seeker," appeared originally in *Evangelical Sacrifices* (1640). Found here in *The Complete Works of Richard Sibbes, D.D.*, vol. 6, *http:// books.google.com/books?id=9dsYAAAAYAAJ&pg=RA2-PA113&lpg=RA2-PA113& dq=richard+sibbes+god+delights+to+spread+his+goodness&source=bl&ots=TBaJ 81NhBy&sig=7ArR9iCiu1LmqnLcHsb_96w3p0M.*

A sample chapter from Pete Gall's
first book *My Beautiful Idol.*

CHAPTER 37

Death of the Hero

Here's the rule for how stories are supposed to go: The hero begins in
his ordinary world, like Frodo living in the Shire or Luke Skywalker
fixing droids in the desert. A crisis is introduced, often by a gate-
keeper character who explains that the hero must leave the ordinary
world to slay a dragon or find a magic elixir or do some other remarkable thing to save the people of the ordinary world. The hero wishes
there could be some other way, but strikes out into the adventure
because there is no other way. Everything rides on the ordinary character successfully performing in the new role of hero.

And Luke Skywalker isn't the only one who performs the role
of hero. We, the audience, also try out the hero's role. We watch the
hero through the lens of our own experiences, and we evaluate how
the hero performs. We see ourselves in that position, and we think
about what we'd do. We practice being heroes for a while.

Once we get a feel for the lay of the land and for the way the
hero tends to respond to the trials he inevitably faces, and once we
know which resources the hero can muster for the fighting of trolls
or stormtroopers or what-have-you, we're ready to set our sights on
the Big Showdown.

Jesus walks around turning water into wine and healing people
and preaching about doing unto others, and we get a sense of what

203

he's like. We see him deliver the smackdown on Peter or the Pharisees here and there.

I get to see myself leave the ordinary world of Chicago and capitalist assumptions. I get to test my clever thoughts about collector crabs and sponge crabs, about me and women and my family and God and how much I pray and what a good boy I can be. I get to learn something about the weapons or resources I can apply in my journey and my battle. I get to see what nice and poetic things I can write and come to understand when my real-life best friend's baby dies, or when a homeless mother of three needs immediate help staying out of the real-life snow, or when I interact with employees or board members or God or demons in the all-too-real night. It's all part of the hoops, all part of preparing for the Big Showdown.

Then the good part comes. We get to see the hero suit up, dig down, kick butt, and push through. We get to see what happens when an ordinary person from the ordinary world leaves the ordinary world to become a hero and then engages an enemy who draws the hero beyond himself. Luke turns off the heads-up display and uses the Force. Frodo is swept to rescue by giant eagles. Jesus didn't "rise" from the dead — he was "raised." Oh, yeah — that's the good stuff. Things will be okay, and the hero will come through. We watch that and we feel better about the chances that we'll come through. God will send his eagles. The Spirit will make fighting Satan feel just like shooting womprats back home in Beggar's Canyon. We want to know it will be okay, and that we will be rewarded by the magic beyond ourselves if we will only keep plugging away until the moment when we reach the end of ourselves and our abilities to fight.

"To thine own self be true."

"God helps those who help themselves."

The list of clichés goes on — our entire worldview is built upon the pattern of the hero's journey. Even our Christianity.

You know why we love the hero's journey pattern so much? We love it because it agrees with our deepest sin and our love for our most beautiful idol: to be our own god. There has been only one hero — and even that hero exists within the enduring mystery of the Trinity. There has been only one hero — and he didn't seek to be his own god. That should be worth more to us than it is.

The hero's journey insists that the pursuit of being our own god will be rewarded by the God we've found a way to accommodate in our idolatry by making him into the one who gets our back when the challenge is too great. We tell the story in a way that assures us he's all about helping us transcend our ordinary world, win the Big Showdown, the BS, and then return as triumphant heroes to the places we once considered quite adequate homes.

We believe in a God who handles the special effects and who would have us be the stars of the show. We love stories like that. We want a God who will make us superhuman, and we don't care much, really, about who he is.

Oh, and here's where the really tasty part comes in. Once God ratifies our status as superhuman, we ascend to a place where "the little people" can no longer understand the mysteries of our greatness. There's nothing more for them to offer us. The Shire has turned foolish and small, and it's ridiculous to think we would submit ourselves to it once again. Those fools in Zionsville could never understand the phenomenal transcendence that comes when a superhuman punk kid gives up selling margarine to watch *Dukes of Hazzard* with retarded guys three days a week. No way — the magic is far too heady for the drones to comprehend. For heroes like we want to be, our only option is to set sail for the faraway magic land of sweet sunsets and rosy syrup. We become gods, and we become free from any accountability — an accountability that would be redundant anyway, since we've become so wise and all that.

We will go through hell itself if we believe that on the far side God will remove the shackles incumbent with our status as contingent beings. As good American Christians we get the added bonus of also having God there to serve us with protection, an ordered universe, and dynamite parking spaces at the mall. That's what a hero is to us, however well we may hide behind coy arguments to the contrary.

Here's what sucks. Frodo Baggins. Luke Skywalker. Me. What do you call someone who leaves the ordinary world on a hero's journey, but fails? What do you say when the Force isn't with you, when the eagles don't show up, or when Melinda dies anyway? There is no such thing as a failed hero. You're either a hero or a failure. Or, as fans of gallant efforts and better luck next time would have it, a fool for believing success was important when it never was. If you die on the way to blow up the Death Star, you fail. If you die on the way to destroy the ring, you fail. If you die on the way to the cross, you fail. And if you fail, you are a failure. And if you are a failure, you don't get to sail away to the land of sweet sunsets and rosy syrup.

That's the problem with the hero's journey. We are all somewhere other than the land of sweet sunsets and rosy syrup. We're all somewhere between the Shire and the pit of fire. We're all somewhere between Tatooine and the Death Star. There's an eagle, but the whole journey's a big, abusive waste of time. The eagle isn't circling, removed and aloof, waiting to pick us up at some location we struggle to reach. The eagle's just as happy to pick us up and take us to the new place from wherever we are.

The only reason it seems like eagles show up at the dramatic climax is that for most of us, it takes a dramatic climax to understand that we're simple hobbits from the Shire with no business tempting such potent enemies.

And the ring? If you ask me, it sounds a lot like the collection on the back of a crab — just a bunch of junk that makes us feel invisible to the bad guys who are only as big a threat to us as we keep them, by our refusal to accept an undeserved rescue from a God who has experienced all of our fear, shame, and sin, and who likes us quite a lot anyway.

This already is the land of sweet sunsets and rosy syrup. The kingdom is among us. We are more than conquerors. This list of worldview-builders goes on and on too. There is a journey for us, and there are trials and challenges, no doubt about that. But what's radically ignored by the world Christians resemble so closely is that our journey begins on the far side of the *Star Wars* credits, or on the page after *The Lord of the Rings* says, "The End."

Success in life is not measured by what we achieve, but by what we come to admit. It is not measured by how far we journey, how many zombies, goblins, or droids we slay, or by our return as champions. It is not measured by how much good I do for any of the people I get paid to care about. Success in life is measured by what we come to admit.

We succeed when we admit we need a ride from an eagle.

We succeed when we admit that we are sinners in the hands of a God who has every right to obliterate us but has instead invited us to journey — to tour — this playground of a planet and this universe of spirit and beauty and joy. We succeed when we admit — as a child admits when she closes her eyes and soaks in her mother's song—that there is nothing for us to do to earn God's love but to receive it.

The point is not the triumph — the point is the deliverance. The point is not the hero — the point is the deliverer.

I want the hero in me to die.

I admit I need my Lord.

Now what?

Share Your Thoughts

With the Author: Your comments will be forwarded to the author when you send them to *zauthor@zondervan.com*.

With Zondervan: Submit your review of this book by writing to *zreview@zondervan.com*.

Free Online Resources at
www.zondervan.com

Zondervan AuthorTracker: Be notified whenever your favorite authors publish new books, go on tour, or post an update about what's happening in their lives.

Daily Bible Verses and Devotions: Enrich your life with daily Bible verses or devotions that help you start every morning focused on God.

Free Email Publications: Sign up for newsletters on fiction, Christian living, church ministry, parenting, and more.

Zondervan Bible Search: Find and compare Bible passages in a variety of translations at www.zondervanbiblesearch.com.

Other Benefits: Register yourself to receive online benefits like coupons and special offers, or to participate in research.